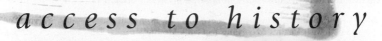

access to history

themes

NATIONALISM
1789–1945

Andrew Matthews

Hodder & Stoughton

A MEMBER OF THE HODDER HEADLINE GROUP

Acknowledgements

The publishers would like to thank the following individuals, institutions and companies for permission to reproduce copyright illustrations in this book:

Sketch by F. Schroeder in the *Dusseldorf Monthly*, Politische Archiv/Auswartiges Amt, Bonn, page 54; 'Jewish Virtues According to Gall's Methods' in *La Libre Parole*, 23/12/1893, The Jewish Museum, New York/John Parkell, page 94; The Imperial War Museum, London, page 109 top and bottom.

The publishers would also like to thank the following for permission to reproduce material in this book:

Arnold for the extracts from *A History of Germany, 1815–1990*, Arnold, 1991; Blackwell Publishers for the extracts from *States, Nations and Nationalism* by H. Schulze, Blackwell, 1996; Cambridge University Press for the extracts from *Nations and Nationalism since 1780* by E.J. Hobsbawm, 1990 and *The European Revolutions, 1848–1851* by J. Sperber, 1994; ITPS Ltd for the extracts from *The Great Powers 1814–1914* by E. Wilmot, Nelson Thornes Ltd, 1992, *Nationalism in Ireland* by D.G. Boyce, Routledge, 1995 and *Ideology and International Relations in the Modern World* by A. Cassels, Routledge, 1996; Extract from *Barricades and Borders. Europe 1800–1914 Second Edition* by R. Gildea, Oxford University Press, 1996, © Robert Gildea 1987, 1996 reproduced by permission of Oxford University Press; Extract from *Oxford History of the French Revolution* by W.O. Doyle, Oxford University Press, 1989, © William Doyle 1989, by permission of Oxford University Press; Pearson Education Ltd for the extracts from *The Origins of the First World War* by J. Joll, Longman, 1992, *The Risorgimento and the Unification of Italy* by D. Beales, Longman, 1981, *France 1814–1914* by R. Tombs, Longman, 1996, *Stalin and Stalinism* by M. McCauley, Longman, 1995 and *Germany 1815–1939* by F. McKichan, Oliver and Boyd, 1992; Verso for the extract by Benedict Anderson: *Imagined Communities* London: Verso 1991, p6.

Every effort has been made to trace and acknowledge ownership of copyright. The publishers will be glad to make suitable arrangements with any copyright holders whom it has not been possible to contact.

Orders: please contact Bookpoint Ltd, 78 Milton Park, Abingdon, Oxon OX14 4TD. Telephone: (44) 01235 827720, Fax: (44) 01235 400454. Lines are open from 9.00–6.00, Monday to Saturday, with a 24 hour message answering service. Email address: orders@bookpoint.co.uk

British Library Cataloguing in Publication Data
A catalogue record for this title is available from The British Library

ISBN 0 340 73782 4

First published 2000
Impression number 10 9 8 7 6 5 4 3 2 1
Year   2005 2004 2003 2002 2001 2000

Copyright © 2000 Andrew Matthews

Cover photo from Private Collection.
Typeset by Fakenham Photosetting Ltd, Fakenham, Norfolk.
Printed in Great Britain for Hodder & Stoughton Educational, a division of Hodder Headline Plc, 338 Euston Road, London NW1 3BH by Redwood Books, Trowbridge, Wilts.

Contents

Preface

The original *Access to History* series was conceived as a collection of sets of books covering popular chronological periods in British history, together with the histories of other countries, such as France, Germany, Russia and the USA. This arrangement complemented the way in which history has traditionally been taught in sixth forms, colleges and universities. In recent years, however, other ways of dividing up the past have become increasingly popular. In particular, there has been a greater emphasis on studying relatively brief periods in considerable detail and on comparing similar historical phenomena in different countries. These developments have generated a demand for appropriate learning materials, and, in response, two new 'strands' have been added to the main series – *In Depth* and *Themes*. The new volumes build directly on the features that have made *Access to History* so popular.

To the General Reader

Access books have been specifically designed to meet the needs of examination students, but they also have much to offer the general reader. The authors are committed to the belief that good history must not only be accurate, up-to-date and scholarly, but also clearly and attractively written. The main body of the text (excluding the Study Guide sections) should therefore form a readable and engaging survey of a topic. Moreover, each author has aimed not merely to provide as clear an explanation as possible of what happened in the past but also to stimulate readers and to challenge them into thinking for themselves about the past and its significance. Thus, although no prior knowledge is expected from the reader, he or she is treated as an intelligent and thinking person throughout. The author tends to share ideas and explore possibilities, instead of delivering so-called 'historical truths' from on high.

To the Student Reader

It is intended that *Access* books should be used by students studying history at a higher level. Its volumes are all designed to be working texts, which should be reasonably clear on a first reading but which will benefit from re-reading and close study.

To be an effective and successful student, you need to budget your time wisely. Hence you should think carefully about how important the material in a particular book is for you. If you simply need to acquire a general grasp of a topic, the following approach will probably be effective:

1. Read Chapter 1, which should give you an overview of the whole book, and think about its contents.
2. Skim through Chapter 2, paying particular attention to the 'Points to Consider' box and to the 'Key Issue' highlighted at the start of each section. Decide if you need to read the whole chapter.
3. If you do, read the chapter, stopping at the end of every sub-division of the text to make notes.
4. Repeat stage 2 (and stage 3 where appropriate) for the other chapters.

If, however, your course demands a detailed knowledge of the contents of the book, you will need to be correspondingly more thorough. There is no perfect way of studying, and it is particularly worthwhile experimenting with different styles of note-making to find the one that best suits you. Nevertheless the following plan of action is worth trying:

1. Read a whole chapter quickly, preferably at one sitting. Avoid the temptation – which may be very great – to make notes at this stage.
2. Study the diagram at the end of the chapter, ensuring that you understand the general 'shape' of what you have read.
3. Re-read the chapter more slowly, this time taking notes. You may well be amazed at how much more intelligible and straightforward the material seems on a second reading – and your notes will be correspondingly more useful to you when you have to write an essay or revise for an exam. In the long run, reading a chapter twice can, in fact, often save time. Be sure to make your notes in a clear, orderly fashion, and spread them out so that, if necessary, you can later add extra information.
4. The Study Guide sections will be particularly valuable for those taking AS level, A level and Higher. Read the advice on essay questions, and do tackle the specimen titles. (Remember that if learning is to be effective, it must be active. No one – alas – has yet devised any substitute for real effort. It is up to you to make up your own mind on the key issues in any topic.)
5. Attempt the source-based questions. The guidance on tackling these exercises is well worth reading and thinking about.

When you have finished the main chapters, go through the 'Further Reading' section. Remember that no single book can ever do more than introduce a topic, and it is to be hoped that, time permitting, you will want to read more widely. If *Access* books help you to discover just how diverse and fascinating the human past can be, the series will have succeeded in its aim – and you will experience that enthusiasm for the subject which, along with efficient learning, is the hallmark of the best students.

Robert Pearce

1 Nationalism: An Introduction to the Key Themes

POINTS TO CONSIDER

This chapter gives an overview of the key developments of the period. The areas identified will be dealt with more fully in subsequent chapters. The key aims for you are therefore to understand the concepts of nation and nationalism and to grasp the main chronological divisions and developments.

1 Introduction

KEY ISSUE Why is nationalism important?

'The most important political fact of the nineteenth century in Europe was the growth of nationalism.'[1] So argues the historian M.S. Anderson and few would disagree. The same could be said of the first half of the twentieth century and, after the events in eastern Europe following the collapse of the Soviet Union, arguably of the second half too. Indeed in Britain issues of nationalism and national identity seem of the utmost contemporary importance, whether we are concerned with the Irish problem, Scottish and Welsh nationalism or our relations with our continental neighbours in the European Union. In addition to this, of course, the people of Europe habitually now describe themselves as British or Italian or French or German or Greek. Nationality helps to define who we are as well as where we come from. However, this was not the case for the vast majority of people two hundred years ago and the history of those centuries is very much the history of how the French became French, the Italians Italian, the Czechs Czech and so on.

The purpose of this book is to outline the history of modern nationalism in Europe from the French Revolution in 1789 through to the end of the Second World War in 1945. It tries to balance developments in specific states against a wider perspective and seeks to assess the impact of nationalism on European history. Tracing this history, however, immediately presents two problems of definition: what is the meaning of the term nation? and, what is the meaning of the term nationalism? Unfortunately the answer to both these questions is not straightforward as the meaning of each term varies both over time and between historians, political scientists and other writers.

2 The Nation

KEY ISSUE What is a nation?

The concept of the nation is a slippery one and any attempt to define
it in more than the most general terms is open to criticism as whatever criteria we apply are unlikely to fit all 'nations'. One such general
definition is given in a recent and influential book on nationalism by
Benedict Anderson. He defines a nation as 'an imagined political
community'. What he means by this is that members of the nation
'will never know most of their fellow-members, meet them, or even
hear of them, yet in the minds of each lives the image of their com-
munion'.[2] It is the belief that we have something in common which
binds all together in a particular national community. It is this sense
of belonging and mutual responsibility, of fraternity, and, of course,
difference from others that arguably made us fight two world wars this
century. But what are the elements that contribute to the making of
this imagined community?

Historians have suggested that two concepts of the nation developed at the end of the eighteenth century: on the one hand, a basi-
cally political definition of the nation and, on the other, an essentially
cultural definition.

a) The Political Nation

This conception of the nation relates to the ideas put forward by J.J.
Rousseau in the 18th century and which were applied in 1789 in the
French Revolution. In his book *The Social Contract* Rousseau argued
that political power (sovereignty) was possessed by the nation, that is
all the people of a particular political community or state. In 1789,
the people of France claimed to be the French nation (rather than
merely the subjects of the king of France) and so claimed that all political power in the state ultimately rested with them. The French
nation wrested political power away from the monarchy and privileged élites. To be French after 1789 was simply to be a citizen of the
French state. The idea of the political nation, then, focuses on a
people's right to self-determination, its right to choose its own government. This idea of the nation has sometimes also been referred to
as the liberal democratic or west European concept.

b) The Cultural Nation

In central and eastern Europe a different concept of the nation developed which did not necessarily have any political overtones. Instead a
nation was defined by reference to a range of criteria such as
common history and culture, common language and religion, and

ties of blood and community derived from long settlement in a particular area. This idea is sometimes referred to as the east-central European concept. Such a checklist, of course, will not fit every case, nor is it meant to – to some nations (such as the Germans) language, history and culture were the defining elements, in others it was religion (such as the Poles). What is important about this concept is that it allowed nations to define themselves without specific reference to an existing state. Germans could see themselves as German without necessarily desiring the creation of a German national state. Similarly Czechs, whilst desirous of cultural recognition and equal opportunities with German citizens, did not for a long time seek autonomy from the Austrian Empire.

Whilst such a distinction is useful, the history of the nineteenth century demonstrates that in the end the two concepts are not mutually exclusive. As cultural nationalism developed in Europe it was quickly linked to political aspirations against existing regimes and, on the other hand, the French quickly began to define themselves in cultural terms. This leads us to the second question:

3 Nationalism

> **KEY ISSUE** What is nationalism?

If it is difficult to define the term nation precisely, it is arguably even more difficult to define nationalism. At the most basic level nationalism refers to the belief that the state and the nation should coincide as in the equation 'people = nation = state'. Indeed nationalists hold that the nation state is the highest, most desirable, and even the only legitimate form of state. Additionally the state in its constitution and actions should reflect the will of the nation. When nation and state do not coincide (as in a multi-national dynastic empire like that of the Habsburgs) the nationalist wants to bring about the nation state; once a nation state exists, the nationalist wants to ensure national unity, to defend the nation state against internal and external threats and to assert national greatness.

But such a definition leaves much unsaid. How, for instance, does one know the 'will of the nation'? A democrat and a fascist would give very different answers. And nationalism developed in a variety of different ways. To some extent the very vagueness of nationalism's meaning has been the secret of its success as a political idea. Nationalism is a political chameleon – at different times, in different places, nationalism has been liberal and conservative, even socialist, progressive and reactionary, democratic and authoritarian, tolerant and intolerant. This is because nationalism itself is not really an ideology like liberalism or socialism, which have a range of interrelated ideas and values.

It does not in itself say much about the nature of the state beyond the idea that its citizenry should comprise the members of the nation.

4 Nationalism 1789–1945: An Overview of Key Themes

> **KEY ISSUE** How did nationalism develop over the period 1789–1945?

a) 1789–1815: The Beginnings of Modern Nationalism

A major result of the French Revolution was the birth of modern nationalism in Europe. The period is important because it indicates many of the developments in nationalism that were to work themselves out in Europe over the succeeding century. In 1789 the people of France, defining itself as the nation, took control of the state and the nation state was created. The sense of nationhood was intensified by the internal attempts to overthrow the revolution and by the experience of war. Victories abroad instilled a sense of national pride and even of national mission, at first the fraternal wish to free other subject peoples but later to civilise Europe by the export of French ideas and by French control of foreign territory.

This last aim was particularly associated with the Napoleonic era (1799–1815). Napoleon argued that he aimed to free Germans and Italians, but whilst he redrew the frontiers of European states, he did little to encourage nationalism directly. Indeed, arguably nationalism developed as a reaction to French rule in the geographical areas of 'Germany' and 'Italy', while a sense of British national identity had begun to develop amongst the masses through the long experience of war with France. In the Italian peninsula and in central Europe there were the first stirrings of nationalism amongst the relatively small numbers of students, academics and middle-class liberals. In central Europe this took a cultural form as writers began to expound the common culture, heritage and language that defined Germans, for example.

b) 1815–1848: The Era of Liberal Nationalism

The key theme in this period is the development of liberal nationalism. The ideas of liberalism and nationalism were closely intertwined in this period. Liberalism can be understood as a political movement which sought to limit the powers of monarchs by means of a constitution which would give a political voice to some (especially the middle classes), if not all, the people of a state and which would guarantee certain rights to the individual. Most states had a system of absolute monarchy which recognised no theoretical limits to the authority of the monarch over his subjects. So liberalism directly challenged an established order that generally refused concessions. This is one reason why liberals were attracted to the French Revolutionary idea of investing political sovereignty in the nation. Liberals began to see, for instance in the possibility of a united Germany or a united Italy, an alternative to the absolutism of a Prussian king or an Austrian Emperor. A German nation had already been identified in cultural terms, now a political shape was given to that cultural nation. Liberals also gave support to the Greeks in their struggle for freedom from the Ottoman Empire.

Economic and social factors, in particular changes associated with industrialisation, urbanisation, railways and a growing middle class, also help explain the growth in nationalism. Indeed many would argue that the formation of a customs union (*Zollverein*) in the German Confederation added economic force to the case for a German nation state.

Elsewhere in Europe, a distinctive nationalist movement led by lesser nobility developed in Hungary and Poland seeking greater self-government within the Austrian and Russian Empires. Academics also began to develop national histories and languages that helped give shape and legitimacy to the claims of other nations – such as the Czechs. More militant nationalists and liberals sought to achieve their aims by revolution. Revolutionary outbreaks occurred in 1820–21, 1830–31 and all across Europe in 1848. They all failed, despite initial success in 1848. This was partly because liberal nationalism enjoyed only limited support amongst a small but growing middle class and because they had insufficient force to achieve their aims.

c) 1848–1878: The Creation of Nation States

The key theme here is the priority that was given to first achieving a nation state, rather than insisting on its liberal character. 1848, if it failed to achieve its liberal nationalist aims, did put the 'principle of nationality' firmly on the political agenda. Nationalists also learnt the lesson that without power little could be achieved. This was the age of *realpolitik,* the politics of realism where to a great degree the end justifies the means. Nationalists looked to Prussia in Germany, Piedmont (with French help) in Italy to achieve their aims. On the other side, Prussia and Piedmont were able to exploit nationalism in pursuit of their aims to dominate Germany and Italy respectively. The loser was the Austrian Empire, which in defeat was forced to compromise with its Hungarian subjects. Elsewhere Balkan nation states were formed on the back of power politics pursued by the Great Powers in relation to the fate of the declining Ottoman Empire. The creation of independent nation states was a way of dealing with the rivalries between Austria and Russia and the other Great Powers who had strategic interests in the area.

d) 1878–1914: Mass Nationalism and the Shift to the Right

By 1878 a number of nation states had been formed across Europe. Although a number of other nationalities still sought 'liberation', or at least recognition from the empires of Austria, Russia and the Ottomans, the key themes of this period are the creation of a mass nationalism in nation states and the exploitation of nationalism by conservative and right-wing forces. Domestically states pursued policies promoting education, the national language and creating national symbols in order to make the nation state the focus of people's loyalty. Conservative forces and the political right also saw nationalism as a means of combating the destabilising politics of socialism (which seemed to threaten the revolutionary overthrow of the established order) and the perceived threat posed by national minorities. The extreme right began to peddle ideas of integral nationalism which sought to place the nation above all other loyalties. International relations were also affected by the development of nationalism. Right-wing nationalists, especially, argued that the acquisition of empire and military might were necessary for national prestige and greatness. Meanwhile, nationalist agitation in the Balkans threatened further break-up of the Ottoman and Austrian empires. Nationalism then played an important role in the origins of the First World War and helps to explain why so many men cheerfully volunteered to fight and die for their country in 1914.

e) 1914–45: Nationalism at its Most Extreme

The victory of the Allies and the ideas of Woodrow Wilson of the USA seemed to presage a new order in Europe based on liberal conceptions of nationalism. A system of nation states buttressed by liberal democratic constitutions and a system of international cooperation via a League of Nations promised a new era of peace and prosperity. It failed. Instead democracy gave way in state after state to some form of right-wing nationalist dictatorship, and nationalism developed its most aggressive and extreme form in Fascist Italy and Nazi Germany. The key theme here then is to explain this shift in nationalism to the extreme right.

   The themes outlined above do not, of course, fit neatly into the time frames indicated. Nationalist movements of liberation, for instance, continued throughout this period and the desire of states to inculcate a sense of national loyalty began as soon as the nation state had come into being. The French experience of 1789–1815 in some ways presages all that followed. What is clear is that nationalism, however disputed its meaning, was a powerful and dynamic force in European history throughout the period from 1789 to 1945. Whether you will agree with M.S. Anderson's conclusion about the nineteenth century is for you to decide having read this book. You may conclude that it could equally apply to the twentieth. Whatever your view, we hope that your conclusions about nationalism will be based on a knowledge and understanding of the facts.

References

1 M.S. Anderson, *The Ascendancy of Europe, 1815–1914* (Longman, 1985), p. 204.
2 B. Anderson, *Imagined Communities* (Verso, 1991), p. 6.

Summary Diagram

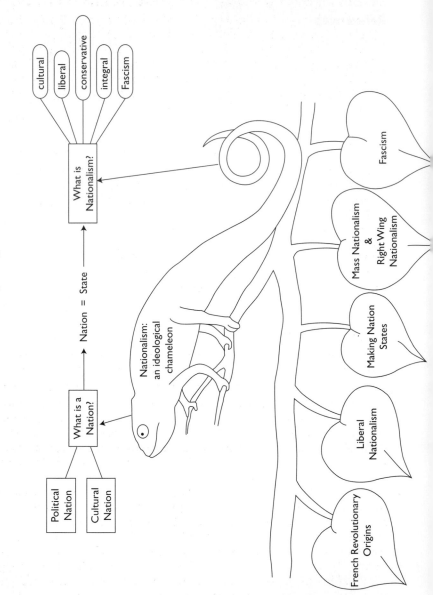

2 The Impact of the French Revolution and Napoleon

POINTS TO CONSIDER

This chapter considers the development of nationalism in France and its impact on Europe during the Revolution and under Napoleon. You will need to focus on understanding the nature of French nationalism and its developing character after 1789, and the development of nationalism outside France. Key distinctions will need to be made between the political nationalism spawned by the French Revolution and the cultural nationalism developing in Germany.

KEY DATES

1789 August	Declaration of the Rights of Man and the Citizen.
1792 April	France declares war on Austria.
September	Battle of Valmy, France declares itself a Republic.
1793 August	*Levée en Masse.*
1799 November	Napoleon seizes power.
1804 December	Napoleon crowns himself Emperor.
1807	Napoleon dominates the Continent.
1812	Napoleon's defeat in Russia.
1815	Vienna Settlement.

1 Introduction

KEY ISSUE What was the political situation in Europe in 1789?

In 1789 the European states system was dominated by the hereditary monarchies of France, the Habsburg Empire (Austria), Prussia, Britain and Russia. Germany did not exist; neither did Italy. Instead each of these areas was divided into a number of smaller states and principalities. For instance, the Holy Roman Empire, headed by the Habsburg Emperor, covered much of central Europe (see the map on page 10) and consisted of over 300 separate kingdoms, ecclesiastical principalities, free cities and petty princedoms. To the south east of Europe lay the Ottoman Empire, dominating the Balkans and the Middle East. The lands controlled by hereditary rulers were theirs by virtue of inheritance, marriage, treaty or conquest. Their claim to rule their subjects was based on notions of divine right. Theoretically answerable only to God, they claimed absolute power over their subjects. However, some had begun to justify their claim to authority in terms of their responsibilities to look after their subjects. Frederick the Great of Prussia (1740-86), for instance, had described himself as the

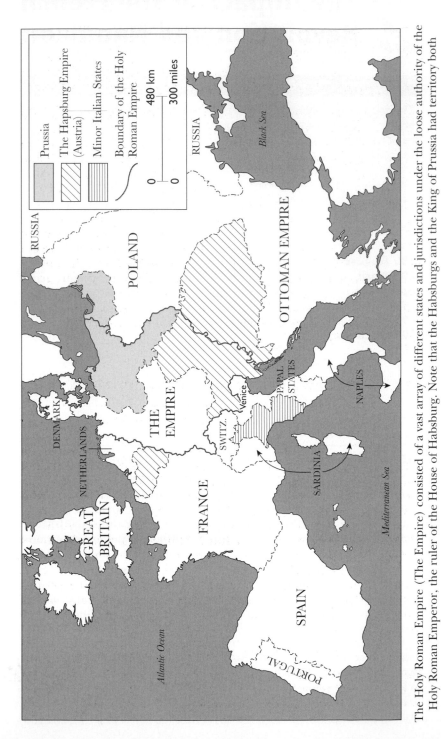

The Holy Roman Empire (The Empire) consisted of a vast array of different states and jurisdictions under the loose authority of the Holy Roman Emperor, the ruler of the House of Habsburg. Note that the Habsburgs and the King of Prussia had territory both inside and outside the Empire.

'servant of his people'. Britain was the fifth great power and the only major constitutional monarchy where the aristocracy and the elected representatives of a small proportion of the population, dominated by the gentry, shared power with the monarch. Of the five major powers only Britain and France were relatively territorially unified.

On the Continent the dominant social system reflected feudal and medieval origins with society divided into three main orders: the clergy, the nobility and the commoners, the vast majority of whom were peasants scratching a living from the soil. Birth or membership to one body or another, be it guild, Church, town, profession or order, determined not only social status but also rights and privileges.

In 1789 this began to change. The French Revolution overthrew the absolute monarchy of Louis XVI and began the process of creating a new social and political order in France. By 1815, no part of Europe was unaffected by its ideas. The Revolution not only swept away the power of kings in France but also redefined the relationship between the individual and society and the individual and the state. Citizens replaced subjects, the interests of the state replaced the whims of monarchs and the idea of the nation state was born. This chapter explores the nature and extent of this transformation and its impact across Europe.

2 The French Revolution and Nationalism

> **KEY ISSUE** How did the French Revolution transform the concept of nation?

Before 1789 the term 'nation' was used, but mainly in reference to what historians call 'the political nation', those whose status and position in society gave them some influence over the direction and governing of the state. That is, it referred principally to the aristocracy. In France, in the months leading up to the tumultuous events of 1789, the term 'nation' was redefined. Abbé Sieyès, a chief publicist and agitator for constitutional reform, in his influential pamphlet entitled 'What is the Third Estate?' (the unprivileged masses), argued that, contrary to contemporary usage, the 'nation' was the people; that the privileged orders (the nobility and clergy) were not part of the nation; and that supreme political authority within the state lay with the 'nation':

The Nation exists before everything, it is the source of everything.[1]

On 14 July 1789, with the Storming of the Bastille, his words were given practical meaning as the people of Paris overthrew absolute monarchy and secured the survival and political supremacy of the newly-established National Assembly, in which the non-privileged order – the Third Estate (dominated by the articulate, professional middle classes) – was the decisive voice. Over the following month this National Assembly began to lay down its revolutionary principles in the Declaration of the Rights of Man and the Citizen (26 August 1789). These drew heavily on the American Declaration of Independence and the ideas of enlightened thinkers like Rousseau. Article 3 reads:

> The source of all sovereignty resides essentially in the nation. No group or individual may exercise authority not derived explicitly from it.

In this short statement the modern idea of a liberal nation state was born – the idea that a state was made up of equal citizens and that within the boundaries of the state these citizens comprised the nation. It also made clear that the source of all sovereignty (political authority) lay in the nation – the citizens of the state. Governments, therefore, were necessarily responsible to the nation or its representatives in a National Assembly. The King was to be known as the King of the French – his kingdom defined by the French people not by mere geography and accidents of inheritance, marriage and conquest. The people were no longer subjects of a King but citizens of France and the King was their servant, there to do the nation's bidding.

In 1789, of course, such notions were revolutionary, and revolutionaries were known as 'patriots', defenders of the nation. Hence there grew in some people's minds the equation between revolution, liberalism and nationalism. It was an association that was to ensure the opposition of conservatives both during and after this period.

However, the definition of 'French' was essentially political; it referred to anyone within the boundaries of the French state; it did not necessarily or explicitly refer to linguistic, or even cultural, heritage. It did not exclude, therefore, German speakers in the east and Basques in the south west; neither did it include the people of the papal territory of Avignon in the south. Indeed there was no linguistic uniformity in France. Breton was spoken in the west, Basque in the extreme south and there was the basic linguistic divide between the 'langue d'oeil' of northern France and the 'langue d'oc' of the south. Linguistic uniformity was to be the creation of the nation state, developing in the wake of the administrative and legal uniformity established by the new regime and a century of state action.

After August 1789 the National Assembly got on with its work of transforming the French state, abolishing feudalism, rationalising administration, reforming finances and the Church, and devising a new Constitution. It was a period of hope and optimism perhaps best demonstrated by the first 'national' holiday – 'La Fête de la Federation' – on 14 July 1790 when National Guardsmen and representatives from all over France gathered in Paris to celebrate the Storming of the Bastille. Unity, freedom and equality were the clarion calls, the themes that bound and defined Frenchmen. From 1789 onwards the adjective 'national' replaced 'royal' in any number of contexts: there was a national guard, a national assembly; the crime of treason was no longer termed *lèse-majesté* but was replaced by the crime *lèse-nation*. The citizen's duty was service to the nation, not obedience to the King.

This was an inward-looking nationalism, concerned with internal arrangements within France, rather than an imperialist, aggressive nationalism. As such it did not appear to offer any real threat to other states, which helps to explain why dynastic states such as Austria and Prussia showed little concern at what was happening in France. Indeed they appeared to welcome the internal problems of France that took this state, temporarily at least, out of the power-politics of Europe.

However, there existed a paradox, for the French Revolution whilst declaring the principle of national sovereignty did so in the name of universal rights. The 'natural rights' proclaimed in the Declaration of the Rights of Man and the Citizen applied to all men, not just Frenchmen. The principles used to justify the overthrow of the privileged orders and absolute monarchy in France could equally well be used to overthrow them elsewhere. Only slowly, however, were the international implications of the new doctrines to become apparent.

Several issues made the Revolution more than just a French affair. These included the following:

i) Foreign radicals
One of the many foreign radicals who came to Paris was the Prussian Anarcharsis Cloots, the self-proclaimed 'orator of the human race'. Cloots' rhetoric spoke of the 'oppressed nations of the universe' who 'sighing equally for liberty would soon break the yoke of the tyrants who oppress them'.

ii) The Church
The logic of Article 3 of the Declaration of the Rights of Man and the Citizen pointed to a re-organisation of the Catholic Church and a requirement that the clergy take an oath of loyalty to the Revolution. Otherwise it would continue to constitute a body claiming to exercise authority within the state without the express authority of the nation. There was, of course, a conflict here, as Catholic clergy owed obedience to the pope. This is one reason why the Civil Constitution of the Clergy (1790) and the associated oath proved so divisive: it forced clergy into a choice half were unwilling to make. The loyalty of that half was immediately suspect and in many revolutionaries' minds Catholicism began to be associated with lack of patriotism and with counter-revolution.

iii) Abolition of feudalism
The idea of a nation state with equal citizens raised questions about the authority of foreign princes who had possessions within France. The National Assembly, of course, believed the peasants on these

lands should enjoy the same rights as other Frenchmen. But, of course, such action had international implications. What if these foreign princes were unhappy, as they were, at these arrangements? By its actions France was making foreign enemies; the Revolution could not be an exclusively French affair.

iv) Émigrés (those, including many aristocrats and royal princes, who had fled and continued to flee, from France after the Revolution)

Many émigrés actively organised counter-revolution and sought the aid of foreign princes. Such agitation of émigrés abroad, in places like Cologne, irritated the new rulers of France who desired foreign princes to withdraw their protection from them. It was this issue that, in 1792, provided the immediate cause of war with the Habsburg Emperor, who was accused of protecting the enemies of France.

v) Marie-Antoinnette and Austria

Marie-Antoinnette, the wife of Louis XVI, had long been portrayed as a villain, a source and symbol of the problems facing France. After the Revolution, not without foundation, she was considered to be working for the restoration of royal power and seeking the assistance of the Habsburg monarchy in the cause. She was also seen as the key player in a so-called 'Austrian Committee' at Court which constantly sought to undermine the work of the Legislative Assembly.

All these issues contributed to the growing concern amongst the dynastic rulers of Europe about the events in France, a concern first given positive, if muted, expression in the Declaration of Pillnitz in the summer of 1791. This declaration by Austria and Prussia expressed hostility to the Revolution and seemed to threaten joint action against France. Thereafter war seemed more likely. In France, in the autumn of 1791, political debate in the newly-elected Legislative Assembly centred on the untrustworthiness of the King, the fear of foreign – and émigré – sponsored counter-revolution and the machinations of the Austrian faction at Court. The result was the declaration of war in April 1792. It was to be a 'defensive' war against the Habsburg Emperor, Francis II, with the aim of maintaining France's 'liberty and independence'. The declaration went on to explain that this was not a 'war of nation against nation, but the just defence of a free people against the unjust oppression of a king. ... The French will never confuse their brothers with their real enemies ...' French nationalism was about to enter a new phase.

3 Nationalism and War

> **KEY ISSUE** To what extent was the nature of French nationalism affected by the experience of war?

This is not the place to give a blow by blow account of the war, but the years 1792–4, when French armies fought desperately to preserve the new France, were a crucial period in the development of nationalism. In a very real sense French national identity was forged on the anvil of war. Up to this point the idea of the nation had been used as a concept to justify the claims of the people against absolute/divine right monarchy and against the privileges of the Church and nobility. From the overthrow of the monarchy in August 1792, the nation – not the monarch – was to be the rallying point for the defence of the Revolution against its enemies. From the gathering of the volunteers from all over France to Paris in the summer of 1792, through the '*levée en masse*' (see page 16) the following year, to the Reign of Terror, a new, militant nationalism grew. French citizens were required to perform the ultimate service to the state: to give up their lives in defence of the nation. The concept of the nation-in-arms was born. The Revolution now had to be fought for and the new France defended. At the same time the fear of counter-revolution and foreign defeat made the revolutionaries uncompromising in the desire for unity and active loyalty to the new France. The Republic of France was 'one and indivisible', the battle-cry was 'liberty or death!' and anyone not enthusiastically 'for' the Revolution was seen as a potential traitor.

Volunteers flocked to Paris in June and July 1792 as the Prussians advanced and Frenchmen responded in droves to the plea to fight in defence of '*la patrie en danger*' in August 1792. At Valmy, on 21 September 1792, the Prussians under Brunswick were defeated. According to legend, it was the enthusiasm of the citizen-soldiers which defeated the enemy; in fact, however, it had rather more to do with what remained of the well-trained artillery of the Ancien Regime. The significance of the event was noted by Goethe, the German Shakespeare: it was the dawning of a new age. The world would never be quite the same again.

The onset of war also spawned new national symbols – most significantly in its songs – most familiarly, the *Marseillaise*, later to become the French national anthem. It is worth examining its words, because they indicate the fervour and new militancy of the Revolution:

1 Come, children of the Motherland, the day of glory has arrived!
  Against us, the tyrant has raised his blood-drenched banner,
  Has raised his blood-drenched banner!
  Don't you hear across our countryside the roar of his merciless soldiery?
5 They are coming right into your arms to butcher your friends and family!
  Citizens, to arms! Form up your battalions!
  Let's march! March! So that our very fields shall wash with their evil blood!
  Wash with their evil blood!

After Valmy French armies went on to push the Austrians back and further victories seemed to confirm the view that the new revolutionary armies inspired by liberty and equality were more than a match for the mercenaries of kings. The wave of optimism that accompanied these victories led to the new Republican assembly, the National Convention, passing the 'Edict of Fraternity' in November 1792:

1 The National Convention declares, in the name of the French Nation, that it will grant fraternity and aid to all peoples who wish to recover their liberty; and it charges the executive power with giving the generals the orders necessary for bringing aid to such peoples, and for
5 defending citizens who have been, or might be, harassed for the cause of liberty.

The French nation now had a national mission – to spread the 'French' doctrines of natural rights and popular sovereignty across Europe. It was the job of the French to civilise Europe. This was to be a feature of French nationalism for the rest of this period. But, as the revolutionary leader of the Terror, Robespierre, put it, no-one likes armed missionaries. Now the French revolution, its fraternity, liberty and equality and its nationalism, was for export – at a price. The costs of liberation were to be met by the freed peoples. They would have to pay for the French armies, contribute to the cause through taxation and provision of supplies and bear the costs of occupation.

The first flush of victories was to be short-lived, however, as the following Spring (1793) France was to be faced by both a hostile Europe-wide coalition and counter-revolution at home. In desperation the National Convention (the new directly-elected assembly in France) turned to Terror, emergency government of a thorough and uncompromising kind, to deal with the situation. For our purposes the most significant element of this was the declaration of the '*levée en masse*' on 23 August 1793. By this decree the 'nation-in-arms' was to become a reality:

1 Henceforth, until the enemies have been driven from the territories of the Republic, the French people are in permanent requisition for army service.

The young men shall go to battle; the married men shall forge arms and
5 transport provisions; the women shall make tents and clothes; the children shall turn old linen into lint; the old men shall stimulate the courage of the warriors and preach the unity of the Republic and hatred of kings.

The levy shall be general. Unmarried citizens or childless widowers
10 from eighteen to twenty-five years shall go first ...

It was this decree which was to unleash the potential of a nation of 28 millions. From this point on national conscription was to provide a seemingly endless resource for the armed forces – in the second half of the 1790s France had around 1 million men under arms. Once more defeat was turned to victory as internal revolt was crushed and

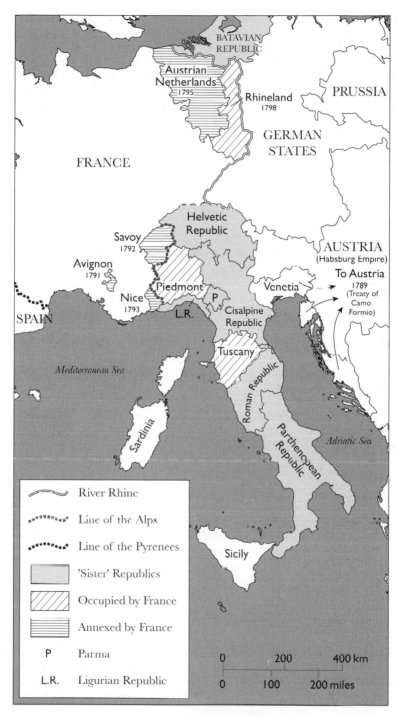

France and Europe in 1799.

foreign enemies were defeated. Once more French armies marched beyond their frontiers, but, in the process, the nature of the war changed. Ostensibly the French were still bringing fraternity and freedom to subject peoples, but the needs of France came first and the attraction of conquest and exploitation threatened to turn the promise of freedom sour. As French armies occupied Belgium, the Rhineland and Savoy, the National Convention in Paris began to talk not of freedom and independence but of annexation and absorption into France. The war of liberation was to become a war of conquest. French nationalism had become aggressive, uncompromising and more or less imperialist.

Between 1792 and 1799 the map of central Europe was re-drawn as France extended its frontiers (see the map on page 17). The new nation, it was argued, should have its borders on its 'natural frontiers' – the Rhine, the Alps and the Pyrenees. Such a doctrine justified the annexation and absorption within France of the Austrian Netherlands, the Rhineland and Savoy, Nice and Piedmont. The fiction of liberation was maintained by claiming the annexations were at the request of the peoples of these areas. In addition, so-called sister republics, in reality client states, had been set up in Holland (Batavian Republic), Switzerland (Helvetic Republic) and Italy. The creation of new states had little to do with realising local aspirations to statehood; the new republics were client states of '*la grande nation*', there to serve the interests of France. As the historian Doyle put it, 'For the Great Nation, however, ... liberty could only be French'.[2]

So, French nationalism had developed from a liberal inward-looking idea in 1789 concerned with the internal arrangements of France, through an outward-looking optimistic nationalism seeking to bring liberation to other subject peoples, to an aggressive, xenophobic, imperialistic version which assumed French superiority. The explanation for this transition is complex. The association of the principle of national sovereignty with universal liberal ideas of equality and natural rights represented a powerful challenge to the existing orders everywhere. The onset of war and internal division made nationalism militant and suspicious, exclusive and xenophobic. Whilst victory seemed to confirm ideological and French superiority, defeat justified the need for greater fervour in defending the Revolution and rigorous measures against those who failed to display it. During the Reign of Terror (1793–4), when the Revolution was under attack from internal and external enemies, suspicion was thrown on any foreigner. It was not just a case of intensified hatred of the Austrians and the English; even a radical like Anarcharsis Cloots was guillotined for his 'foreign' background. Meanwhile fears for national security added weight to arguments for 'natural frontiers' and 'sister republics'. Moreover as time passed national pride began to require '*la gloire*' and the nation-in-arms with its able young generals like Napoleon Bonaparte could provide it. The French Revolution was exported, but all exports had to be paid for. The price of freeing 'subject peoples' was high and the realities of war meant plunder and exploitation of 'liberated' areas. War had to pay for war and if possible yield a profit to France. In this way the interests of the France took precedence over liberty, fraternity and equality abroad. Even so liberalism and French nationalism were not mutually exclusive. Even when French armies moved on to conquest and annexation the principles of the Rights of Man followed.

4 Ireland and Poland

> **KEY ISSUE** How far did the example of France stimulate the growth of nationalism elsewhere in Europe?

In two areas not occupied by France, in Poland and Ireland, those wishing liberation from 'foreign' rule were given some encouragement. Poland had practically disappeared from the map in the partitions of 1772 and 1793. In 1794 Polish nobles and others, resentful of foreign rule (principally by Russia), attempted to rise under the leadership of Kosciuszko. He had sought French aid but received little more than sympathetic noises and words of encouragement. However, faced by the ambitions of Prussia, Russia and Austria, the Polish insurrection was crushed bloodily. In the subsequent partition what remained of Poland disappeared from the map. The desire for an independent Poland did not die, however, and the Poles were to see in Napoleon a means to achieve their aim (see page 23).

In Ireland the desire to loosen ties with Britain had begun to revive during the American War of Independence (1776–83), but the French Revolution gave it a new stimulus and in 1791 a new organisation called the United Irishmen was formed to work for some kind of independence. Limited concessions towards legislative independence had been achieved in1782, but the United Irishmen wanted more. Their aims were:

> ... to unite the whole people of Ireland, to abolish the memory of all past dissensions, and to substitute the common name of Irishmen in place of the denominations of Protestants, Catholic, Dissenter.[3]

However, despite the hopes of leaders like Wolfe Tone, himself a Protestant by background, Irish nationalism, in contrast to the French, was most closely linked with Catholicism.

In 1795, dreaming of independence, the United Irishmen worked to create a network of supporters across the country which sought to tap into the social and economic distress of rural Ireland. Their leaders looked to France for aid. But French policy was dictated not so much by desire to see an independent Ireland as by the chance to distract and harm Britain, with whom she was at war. A French force did arrive in 1798, but only after the uncoordinated and limited Irish rebellion had been crushed in the Battle of Vinegar Hill. The 'hero' of Irish nationalism, Wolfe Tone, was captured and committed suicide. Despite this rising, Irish nationalism in the 1790s remained weak and the idea of an independent Ireland the dream of a few; the real threat to British dominance was relatively modest. However, the rising had frightened the government and Pitt, the British Prime Minister, sought to strengthen British influence whilst at the same time making concessions to Catholics in his proposals for a reformed union. In the event, the Act of Union (1800) abolished the Irish Parliament without granting concessions and Irish nationalism had to wait for Daniel O'Connell to re-awaken it in the 1820s.

5 Napoleon and Nationalism

> **KEY ISSUE** To what extent did Napoleon encourage the growth of nationalism?

Napoleon Bonaparte came to power in France in a coup d'état in November 1799. He was to take the French army to heights of military glory between 1805 and 1807 and to the depths of despair in 1812; he was to subjugate most of the European continent and bring order and stability to France; he was to be defeated in 1814 only to return in 1815 for a brief Hundred Days before defeat once more at Waterloo. He had great influence in shaping the development of French nationalism and arguably did much to stimulate nationalism elsewhere, whether by intention or not.

a) France

The centralised state was a feature of the France of the Reign of Terror; it was also the system adopted by Napoleon. The Abbé Sieyès, who helped Napoleon into power, spoke of 'Authority from above, confidence from below'. Historians have described his rule as 'dictatorship by plebiscite'. This is because he sought popular consent for his regime in more or less engineered plebiscites, such as that held to endorse his adoption of the imperial title in 1804. Napoleon believed popular sovereignty lay in governing the people as they wished to be governed – and he believed he had a particular insight into the people's wishes. In his mind (as in the minds of twentieth century dictators) the interests of the state were the interests of Napoleon: Louis XIV's claim '*L'état, c'est moi*' ('I am the state') could, perhaps, more appropriately apply to Napoleon. Napoleon wished to rise above the factionalism and struggles between the revolutionaries and royalists of the 1790s and to bring order and stability to France. He was, there-fore, less interested in what a person's ideological history was than in his willingness to serve the state – to serve France. Hence his admin-istration contained seemingly incompatible members including regi-cides, ex-royalists and moderates of all colours. His administration also developed a duty of service to the state, to France and to French national interests, which in the end overrode any personal loyalty to himself. This partly explains why Napoleon began to lose the support of important servants after around 1807. Talleyrand, his foreign min-ister, for instance, left Napoleon's service when he believed Napoleon's policies became personal and divorced from the real interests of France. It is also one factor in explaining why the admin-istrative transition from Napoleon to a restored Bourbon monarchy in 1815 was so smooth. Such a commitment to service, to a 'national interest' that must come before personal loyalties, is a feature of modern nation states. It was a feature of French nationalism which was to develop through the nineteenth century.

In Napoleonic France, as in the Reign of Terror, the national interests of France could override the individual rights of Frenchmen; these interests – order, stability, the requirements of the war effort – could be used to justify censorship and the suspension of normal civic rights for political suspects. In this way the direct link between nation-alism and the 'rights of man' was arguably broken – liberalism and nationalism were not necessarily inter-linked. In an emergency, at any rate, liberal ideals could be sacrificed in the interests of national security.

b) Did Napoleon Encourage Nationalism?

In exile on St Helena after 1815, Napoleon was to claim that he sup-ported the aspirations of nations to independence:

> There are scattered over Europe more than 30 million French, 15 mil-lion Spanish, 15 million Italians, and 30 million Germans. My intention was to make each of these peoples into a separate national state.

Is there any truth in this claim? In relation to Italy Napoleon said:

> 1 It was my desire to raise the Italian nation from its ruins: to unite once more the Venetians, Piedmontese, Genoese, Milanese, Tuscans, Parmesans, Modenese, Romans, Neapolitans, Sicilians, and Sardinians in one independent nation, bounded by the Alps and the Adriatic, Ionian
> 5 and Mediterranean seas; such was the immortal trophy which I was rais-ing to my glory. This great and powerful kingdom would have been, by land, a check to the House of Austria, while by sea its fleets, combined with those of Toulon, would have ruled the Mediterranean and pro-tected the ancient road of Indian commerce by the Red Sea and Suez.
> 10 ... But I had many obstacles to surmount. I said ...: 'It will take me twenty years to re-establish the Italian nation'.[4]

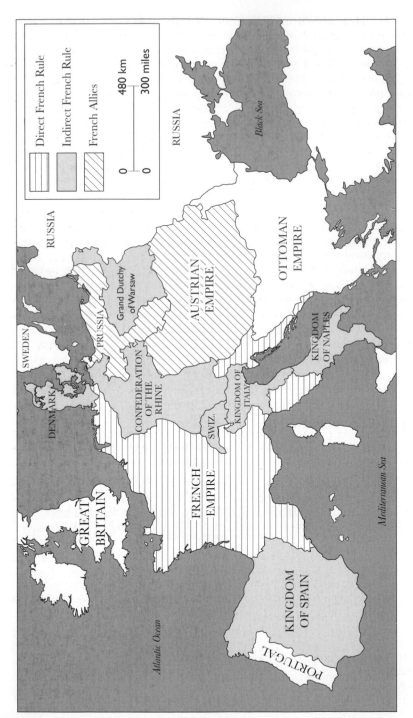

Europe in 1810.

These claims are worth examining. Certainly Napoleon from the very start displayed no hesitancy in seeking to reorganise the Italian state system – Savoy and Nice were annexed, the Cisalpine and Ligurian republics were created, Venice was ceded to Austria by the Treaty of Campo Formio in 1797; later the Kingdom of Italy and the Kingdom of Naples were set up (see map on page 22). There was as a consequence a good deal of administrative reorganisation: administrative systems copied more or less the French approach, the French civil law code, the *Code Napoleon*, was exported and customs regulations were simplified. However, it is also clear that the reorganisations of states and the re-drawing of boundaries were carried out to serve the interests of France and Napoleon: the Italian provinces were ruthlessly exploited to help supply and finance the French war machine. The new states were to be client states of France and became enmeshed in Napoleon's attempt to create a dynastic empire. So the Kingdom of Naples went first to his brother Joseph and thence to his brother-in-law Murat. Indeed some of mainland Italy was absorbed directly into the French Empire. What is more, radicals were censored and suppressed. A careful reading of Napoleon's memoirs indicates that he was determined to ensure that whatever Italian state did emerge would be subservient to French interests. Whether Napoleon did in the long term envisage a re-established Italian state remains uncertain, but the obstacles in its way were huge and Napoleon was preoccupied elsewhere.

Napoleon made similar claims about Germany and a similar story emerges here – the Holy Roman Empire disappeared in 1806 and the chaotic system of over 300 states, princedoms, ecclesiastical principalities and free cities was rationalised. As in Italy new kingdoms were created (such as Westphalia) and some parts were absorbed directly into the Empire (such as the Rhineland). Older states were rewarded for their loyalty by expansion (as in Bavaria) and a new federation established (the Confederation of the Rhine) (see the map on page 22). As in Italy the *Code Napoleon* was exported, administrative systems were reorganised on French lines, and customs regulations were simplified. But, as in Italy, it is hard to see in all this some plan to create a German nation state; the aim was rather to provide reliable allies on the borders of France and territories to be exploited for the benefit of France and her armies.

The Poles, as they had in the 1790s, continued to look to France for support to create an independent Poland, and Polish regiments proved some of Napoleon's most reliable. The achievement of their aim seemed within reach when Napoleon decisively defeated first the Austrians(1805), then the Prussians (1806), and forced the Russians to terms at Tilsit (1807). The powers that had divided Poland between them were all now defeated, and, furthermore, Napoleon was in love with his Polish mistress, Marie Waleska, Countess of Warsaw. The Grand Duchy of Warsaw was created. But was this to be the vehicle of

Polish national aspirations? No! Despite Napoleon's warm words and vague promises to the Poles, far from being an independent Poland, this was yet another client state to be ruthlessly exploited for French purposes. Polish lands were used as rewards for marshals, while Polish subjects were conscripted for service in the army and taxes levied on them to pay for the French war effort. The Grand Duchy was a hollow creation and Polish aspirations remained unfulfilled.

Abroad, in the client and allied states, French interests still came first. All client states had to provide resources, men and finance for the French war effort. There is then little to support the contention that Napoleon deliberately fostered and encouraged nationalism with a view to creating a Europe of independent nation states.

c) Did Nationalism Arise in Resistance to Napoleon?

Many historians have pointed out that what nationalism existed in the Napoleonic period was developing in opposition and resistance to the French; it was not the product of Napoleon's positive encouragement. Yet one must be careful here not to confuse nationalism (in the sense of the desire to create a nation state of equal citizens) with more traditional popular resistance to foreign oppression. In Spain, for instance, the long, sporadic war against France combined traditional loyalties to Church and King with traditional resistance to economic exactions. Priests since the 1790s had preached that the French revolutionaries were atheists and therefore to be detested and a foreign-imposed monarch and an army of occupation was less acceptable than Spain's hereditary monarchy, however flawed. Again much Spanish resistance was local and regional rather than national and many of the guerrilla bands that did emerge were little more than brigands who attacked both French and Anglo-Portuguese forces. If to be Spanish was to be Catholic, then to be Russian was to be Orthodox. The same traditional loyalties and resistance to the depradations of an invading army stimulated opposition in Russia in 1812.

More significant were the stirrings of nationalism in Germany and Italy. The historian Adrian Lyttleton has suggested that 'the Italian question did not exist as a political reality before 1796'.[5] Before Napoleon's invasion in 1796 there is little evidence of any desire for a united Italian state. It was Italian sympathisers with the French Revolution who first defined the idea of a united Italy as a concrete aim. The influence of the French revolution meant that at this stage Italian nationalism found expression in the idea of an association of free citizens who were free from oppression. The poet-nationalist Alfieri, therefore renounced his status as a subject of the King of Piedmont-Sardinia to illustrate his claim to be a free citizen. Nationalists were given heart as the old order crumbled under the Napoleonic onslaught and Italian intellectuals wrote essays on the form the new Italy should take, suggesting, for instance, either a federation recognising regional differences or a unitary Republic. But France was not interested in creating an Italian state. Instead it looked to exploit Italian wealth. Napoleon, for example, showed scant regard for Italian sensibilities in his negotiations with the Austrians resulting in the Treaty of Campo Formio (1797), which transferred Venice to them. Some Italian nationalists, therefore, began to recognise the hollowness of French promises of 'fraternity', but others still saw France as the only hope.

When Austrian armies swept through Italy in 1799 driving out the French, the absence of popular nationalistic fervour was evident: the Austrians were welcomed in Lombardy, and in the south the Parthenopean Republic (Naples) was swept away by a popular insurrection. Nationalists – mainly intellectuals – still saw the French as the lesser of two evils and, after Napoleon's defeat of the Austrians at Marengo in 1800, sought to achieve what self-rule they could from the French leader. Despite the aspirations of nationalists like Melzi who hoped to create a sense of nationhood through efficient government, the subordination of Italy to French needs – especially through taxation and conscription – ensured popular peasant hostility.

Britain had hoped to exploit Italian national feeling in leading resistance to Napoleon in 1814, but these efforts met with only muted response. But perhaps the lack of a nationalist movement is best demonstrated by the failure of Murat, Napoleon's King of Naples, to rouse Italians to fight against the Austrians for independence during the Hundred Days in 1815.

In Germany, that assortment of states that occupied central Europe north of the Alps, there were signs of a developing national consciousness, at least among the educated elites, in the late eighteenth century. This had begun independently of the French Revolution but was given new vigour in reaction to it and the exploitation of Napoleon. The cultural nationalism that had begun to develop in Germany with its interest in the history and folk memory of the *Volk* (loosely translated as the 'people'), however, did not imply the development of a nation state. But the appeal to 'Germans' (a people united by culture and history) could be invoked against the French. The defeat of Prussia at Jena-Auerstadt in 1806, in particular, was, as Hagen Schulze has put it, 'the first spark which set German nationalism alight'.[6] Whilst the 'War of Liberation', insofar as it refers to a popular uprising against Napoleon and the French, may be a myth, there was certainly an attempt to galvanise support by such an appeal. This had begun as early as 1809 when, stimulated by Spanish resistance, the Austrians once more decided to take up arms. They hoped to win support from other German states and peoples, which is why Schlegel was commissioned to write an *Appeal to the German Nation*. The appeal fell flat. 'Germany' did not rise, and the Austrians were defeated at Wagram (July, 1809).

However, intellectuals like Fichte, Jahn and Arndt began to influence the bourgeoisie and students in Germany. Fichte's 'Lectures to the German Nation' in 1807–8 in Berlin met with an enthusiastic response; Jahn's German League of 1810 and his Gymnastics Society of 1811 were significant if small signals of a changing consciousness. All three gave German resistance to the French a kind of mystical, almost religious quality. In the words of the poet Arndt:

> Let the unanimity of your hearts be your church, let hatred of the French be your religion, let freedom and fatherland be your saints, to whom you pray![7]

By the time of Napoleon's humiliation in Russia (1812), a political atmosphere was developing in which an appeal to the German nation would meet a significant response at least amongst the educated middle classes and artisans of Prussia and north Germany. Frederick William III of Prussia was finally persuaded to take up arms against Napoleon in 1813 and issued an appeal calling on 'Prussians and Germans' to fight. While peasants remained largely immune to such appeals, volunteer units were formed from students and artisans. Their songs spoke of the 'fatherland' and 'freedom'. There was no aspiration to a German state in this, more a hatred of the French and an association with a 'German nation' determined by a common language and culture. This linguistic and/or cultural criterion was, however, to play a significant role in the development of nationalism in the nineteenth century, especially in those areas subject to 'foreign' rule, like Italy, or in those areas with several different states like 'Germany'. The emphasis on a common language, history or culture helped to emphasise what united people in these areas when so much else divided them – rulers, social status, rights and privileges.

d) British Nationalism and the Wars Against France

The most consistent enemy of both revolutionary France and of Napoleon was Great Britain. Indeed the most consistent enemy of France for the whole of the eighteenth century was Britain. Between 1793 and 1815 there was effectively just one brief respite in 1802-3 when France and Britain were at peace. What impact did these years of war have on the creation of a British national consciousness? The answer is not straightforward, for unlike the lands of central Europe Britain had enjoyed a relative territorial unity as a state ever since the start of the seventeenth century and its island status gave it a clear geographical cohesion. Its domestic history was therefore somewhat isolated from the continent, a factor reinforced by the Protestantism of its people. Arguably there existed a British nationalism amongst the political élite before the French Revolution based around this Protestantism, around Britain's constitutional monarchy and the idea of British 'freedoms' (developed since the Reformation of the sixteenth century and through the internal revolutions of the seventeenth). Its definition and its spread through the population as a whole was, however, partly forged by war. Linda Colley has charted this development of national identity and argues that the twin agents of war and Protestantism were crucial in binding Englishmen, Scotsmen and Welshmen together in a common sense of British nationhood. In this, rivalry with and enmity for the (Catholic) French played a key role; the war against revolutionary France and Napoleon intensified and developed this sense of nationhood not only amongst the ruling classes but amongst many ordinary people as well. Whilst radical ideas made some headway amongst artisans in London, Sheffield and Norwich in the 1790s, the government could to a great degree rely on the 'Church and King' sympathies of the masses to oppose the 'foreign' ideas proposed by radicals. Over 22 years the demands of war (taxes, military service, disruption of economic life) intruded on all people's lives and gave them a common experience. The fight against a common enemy reinforced recognition of what Scots, Welsh and English had in common. In this sense a British 'national consciousness' developed. In the upper and middle classes, such consciousness was represented in a belief in the worth, even superiority of, the values and institutions of the British state (such as parliament, the monarchy, British 'freedom' and the Protestant faith). How far such beliefs penetrated the working classes is harder to establish, but Linda Colley has shown there was much active 'patriotism' amongst ordinary men and women during the French Revolutionary and Napoleonic Wars.

At this point it is worth emphasising a peculiarity of British nationalism throughout the period covered by this book. The United Kingdom combined four national groups – English, Scottish, Welsh and Irish. Except in the last case, and even here not amongst the Anglo-Irish aristocracy, by the nineteenth century people generally viewed themselves, and others viewed them, as simultaneously Scottish and British, Welsh and British, or English and British. Indeed, amongst the political élite, the terms British and English, Britain and England were used interchangeably. England was a synonym for Britain and the British Empire was also the Empire of England.

6 Conclusion: Nationalism and the Vienna Settlement

KEY ISSUE How far had nationalism developed in Europe by 1815?

Whatever stirrings of nationalism there were in central Europe in the final years of the Napoleonic adventure, and despite efforts made to exploit these feelings by the Great Powers, they were ignored totally when the peacemakers gathered at Vienna to re-draw the map of Europe once more. The issues of interest to them were how to contain France; how to re-establish a reasonable balance of power; how to compensate each other for exchanges of territory; how to accommodate their respective territorial ambitions; and, finally, whether to restore 'legitimate' monarchs. The effects of Napoleon and the need to contain France meant there could be no straightforward return to the arrangements of 1789 and the new states' system of 1815 was a simpler system than that of the eighteenth century. 'Italy' was now simplified into eight main states, dominated by Austria; 'Germany' was re-organised into the German Confederation of 39 states; Belgium joined the Netherlands in a short-lived new state; and 'Poland' was effectively dominated by Russia.

Many late nineteenth century historians, commenting at a time when a united Germany and a united Italy had been created, criticised the peacemakers at Vienna for ignoring nationalism, and there was even some contemporary criticism along these lines from MPs in the House of Commons in 1815. But in most of Europe at this time there was little widespread sense of nationalism or belief in the idea that nations, be they peoples with similar cultural or linguistic heritages or inhabitants of a particular area, should necessarily correspond to states. Furthermore, the continental monarchies which had fought revolutionary France and Napoleon were hardly likely to espouse ideas that they associated with revolution, violence and war, and which threatened their very existence. Nationalism not only threatened to break up old empires like that of the Habsburgs, it was, also, closely associated in rulers' minds – and in reality – with liberalism, a doctrine which would involve the surrender of absolute power, the granting of constitutions, acceptance of civil equality – in short, with political and social revolution. As Metternich, the Austrian Foreign Minister (1809–48), put it: 'Two words suffice to create evil ... the words are liberty and equality'.

By 1815, then, nationalism had become established in France and had begun to develop in a number of continental states and regions, but it can hardly yet be described as a dominant force. Despite Napoleon, it was strongly linked to notions of liberalism and in many ways in the first half of the nineteenth century should be seen as its junior partner. The concept of a state comprising a nation of equal citizens had been born. But the expansionist ambitions of France in the late 1790s and Napoleon had shown that nationalism and liberalism were not totally interlinked. Whilst citizenship in legal terms might be implied, this did not necessarily extend to political rights – to freedom of the press or democracy. However, many of those who were to argue, rebel and fight for a nation state in the generation after Waterloo wanted primarily to see liberal reforms, and saw the creation of a united Germany or united Italy as the means to gain constitutional and responsible government in the face of a hostile existing order.

Within France, arguably, a sense of national consciousness had penetrated the masses, especially in the towns and cities. Its features included a commitment to constitutional government, to a constitution that guaranteed equality before the law and other rights, and a strong sense of national pride and desire for '*la gloire*'. The uniform systems of government and the centralised state helped to bind Frenchmen together. On the continent outside France, however, nationalism was, like liberalism, largely confined to the professional and educated middle classes and a few 'enlightened' members of the aristocracy. In Germany, for instance, it amounted to little more than vague aspirations and a sense of cultural community within academic circles. But, however limited, its presence amongst the articulate and progressive classes meant it represented a potentially powerful threat to the traditional authorities. The significance of the Wartburg Festival of 1817, celebrating the tercentenary of the German Reformation and the anniversary of the 'Battle of the Nations', was not lost on Metternich, who sought the earliest opportunity to stifle such stirrings of German liberal nationalism.

The French political conception of nationalism as defined in the Declaration of the Rights of Man and the Citizen suggested that everyone within the political boundaries of a state comprised the 'nation'. They were 'citizens' of a 'state', not subjects of a king, and ultimate political power resided in this 'nation'. Governments therefore were legitimate only insofar as they were accepted by the 'nation'. At the time this was taken to mean that government had to be answerable to the citizens through some kind of elected assembly. However, Napoleon claimed that national sovereignty could be demonstrated by governing the people as they would wish to be governed – that is, it was possible for one person to know this without recourse to elected assemblies. The link to liberal notions of constitutional government could therefore be divorced from the concept of the nation state. This breaking of the link between liberal notions of 'rights' and nationalism was also demonstrated in the Reign of Terror. 'National interest' could override the 'rights' of an individual; in an emergency such as civil or foreign war, the needs of the 'republic' required the suspension of normal civil rights.

Furthermore, the exploits of the French during this period demonstrated also how nationalism could become aggressive and imperialist. Just as 'national interest' could justify suspension of individual rights, so it could justify overriding the 'rights' of other states and nations. French nationalism implied superiority over others – the French were '*La Grande Nation*' with a mission to civilise the world.

The French concept of nationalism did not necessarily imply a necessity for a common linguistic or cultural heritage. But this was to become another 'test' of nationality. Language and culture were to become a feature of French nationalism in the nineteenth century. They were also a feature of the justification of many other nineteenth century nationalist movements. Such an emphasis can be seen in the first stirrings of German and Italian nationalism during this period although such cultural nationalism was not at this stage necessarily linked to a desire for a nation state.

If the revolutionary and Napoleonic period, then, had not seen a massive eruption of nationalist fervour across Europe, it had laid the seeds for future growth and did provide some powerful images on which nationalists everywhere could call. Poles would look back at Napoleon as a hero; Germans under Willliam II in the 1890s would look back to Frederick William's appeal to 'Prussians and Germans' and the 'War of Liberation'; the Spanish would celebrate the 'Dos de Mayo' rising against the French; the Russians would recall 1812; the British would similarly recall Trafalgar and Waterloo (as late as the 1980s Mrs Thatcher proposed reviving Trafalgar Day as an alternative to the 'socialist' May Day Bank holiday); for Italians the period after 1796 marks the first stirrings of the *risorgimento,* or resurgence of national feeling, which would eventually result in the creation of an Italian state; Wolfe Tone and Vinegar Hill would enter the hagiography of Irish nationalism. So whilst not creating mass nationalism, this period became a potent source of nationalist myths, of stories to encourage a national consciousness.

So, many of the fundamental questions which would face nationalists in the succeeding two centuries had been raised by the course of events between 1789 and 1815. Two hundred years later, most of the same questions are still with us. Did the relationship 'nation = state = people' necessarily imply the liberal solution of popular sovereignty expressed through some kind of representative government, as in France between 1789 and 1792? Or could one man (like Napoleon) know the 'national interest' without recourse to democratic institutions? Should the needs of the 'nation' be used to override the rights of the individual or groups within society, as the Reign of Terror had demonstrated? Should loyalty to the nation or state come before other loyalties, as Napoleon had suggested? Could nations live happily alongside each other recognising each nation's right to determine its own future, as the Edict of Fraternity had seemed to imply? Or were a sense of innate superiority, xenophobia and aggression necessarily linked to the growth of national spirit, as the French experience seemed to demonstrate? Should an awareness of 'national consciousness', as had begun in Germany, necessarily lead to desire for a nation state? These are all themes which arose in the course of European history in the years after 1815 and which will be examined in subsequent chapters.

References

1 As quoted in Liah Greenfeld, *Nationalism: Five Roads to Modernity* (Harvard, 1992), p. 172.
2 W.O. Doyle, *Oxford History of the French Revolution* (Oxford, 1989), p. 353.

3 As quoted in D.G. Boyce, *Nationalism in Ireland* (Routledge, 1995), p. 127.
4 Ed. Somerset de Chair, *Napoleon on Napoleon, An Autobiography of the Emperor* (Cassell, 1992), pp. 193–4.
5 A. Lyttleton, 'The National Question in Italy', in *The National Question in Europe in Historical Context*, edited by M. Teich and R. Porter (Cambridge, 1993), p. 63.
6 Hagen Schulze, *The Course of German Nationalism* (Cambridge, 1991), p. 49.
7 Schulze, *The Course of German Nationalism*, p. 50.

Summary Diagram

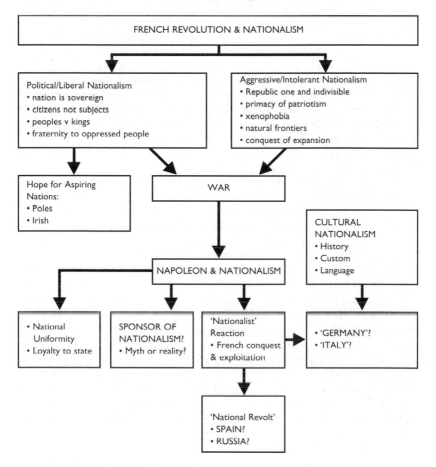

Answering source-based questions on Chapter 2

a) Look at the extract from the *Marseillaise* on page 15. What does the language and tone of this song tell you about the nature of French national feeling in 1792? (*5 marks*)

b) Look at the extract from the *levée en masse* on page 16. How far can this source be seen as a declaration of 'total war' by the French nation? (*5 marks*)

c) Look at the extract from the edict of Fraternity on page 16 and the extract from Napoleon's memoirs on page 21. In the light of these sources and your own knowledge examine the claim that the French Revolutionaries and Napoleon wanted to liberate subject peoples in Europe. (*10 marks*)

Advice: Question a) is asking you to look closely at the words of the source. Students often fail to read sources carefully and yet the utility of a source will depend on a clear understanding of its meaning. When thinking about tone and language, consider whether the language is sober and rational or emotive and passionate? Look closely at the use of adjectives and adverbs and the impact they are likey to have on the reader/singer. What is the message of the source? In answer to questions like this do not be afraid to quote from the source.

Question b) is about understanding the meaning of the source and its historical context by testing it against a relevant concept. Clearly your answer will depend on your definition of the term 'total war'. You must, however, look closely at what the source says and place it in its correct historical context. Knowledge of the historical context will help you to interpret the meaning of the source more effectively.

Lots of source questions, like question c), ask you to test what they say against your own knowledge. Here you need to think about the nature of the sources. What do the sources say? Are they statements about what happened or merely intentions? Are they good evidence of genuine motives or not? Are the motives they reveal supported by the evidence?

Answering essay questions on Chapter 2

Consider the following essay titles:

1. 'Talk of liberation was merely the excuse for foreign conquest.' How far do you agree with this assessment of French aims abroad in the period 1792–1799?

2. To what extent and why did nationalism in Europe grow in the period 1799–1815?

Both these questions seek an evaluation of the issue raised in the question. Question 1 requires an analysis of French aims abroad after war broke out in 1792. The quotation is there to help you to shape your analysis. It suggests that there were two potential aims – liberation and conquest. One useful approach in planning your answer would be to research the evidence for and against the notion of 'liberation' and for and against the notion of 'conquest'. You will then be able to decide where the balance lies. The answer might be different, for example, in relation to 1792–93 than to 1796–97. Was there, for instance, some genuine desire to 'free' subject peoples from their absolute monarchies, or was this always a gloss for more cynical motives of conquest? Question 2 is more open and requires both an assessment of the degree to which nationalism grew and also an explanation for that growth. Be careful in such questions to ensure you address both elements. Relevant issues to consider include: where can nationalism be said to have developed in this period? Was the pattern common across the continent? Or was the development more significant in some areas than others? Was nationalism stimulated by Napoleon or did it rather arise in reaction to him and his conquests?

3 National Awakenings, Europe 1815–48

POINTS TO CONSIDER

This period saw the development of liberal nationalism amongst the educated and middle classes of central Europe. You will need to focus on the nature of liberal nationalist movements, how far they represented a challenge to the existing regimes and why nationalist revolutions in 1848 failed to produce nation states.

KEY DATES

1815	Vienna Settlement.
1819	Karlsbad Decrees stifle liberal/nationalist activity in German Confederation.
1820–21	Revolutions in Italy and Spain. Rebellion in Greece.
1829	Greece wins independence.
1830	Revolution in France.
1839	Belgian independence recognised.
1840	Rhine Crisis stimulates German Nationalism.
1848	Revolutions across Europe with some temporary success.

1 Starting Points: 1815

> **KEY ISSUE** What are the characteristics of a nation?

In 1815 the political organisation of most of Europe was not based on nationality (see the map on page 42). For example, as a result of the Vienna Settlement, Italy was left divided into eight different states dominated by the Bourbons in the south and the Austrian Habsburgs in the north; and, to the north of the Alps, the German Confederation was no more than a loose association of absolute rulers. Dynastic empires, such as Russia and Austria, and hereditary monarchies were once again triumphant and the conservative powers of the Holy Alliance – Austria, Prussia and Russia – were committed to intervening to restore monarchs overthrown by revolution and were determined to repress any nationalist, liberal or radical activity.

But nationalism was not dead. The ideas spawned by the French Revolution could not be destroyed. By 1848 there were nationalist movements across Europe, from the Irish to the Rumanians and from the Danes to the Croats, and two new nation states had been created in Greece and Belgium. Then in 1848 nationalist revolutions broke out across the continent. It seemed the old order was at an end. However, in the event, the old order fought back and none of the revolts succeeded in establishing a new nation state.

What is a nation? There is no straightforward answer as each national movement developed in its own particular historical context and emphasised different features that contributed to the nation's unique identity. Nations had to be made, almost to be invented, by nationalists. There is no set recipe, but national movements identified some or all of the following characteristics:

- a common language: the establishment of a national language was to become the hallmark of the nation state;
- a common religion: in some cases religion was a key element in binding a people together;
- a shared history: in developing national awareness academics sought to discover their nation's history and the roots of their common culture. They sought to establish the elements of a people's shared past which had shaped its development;
- a common state: some nationalists could look to a present or past kingdom or state as the basis of their national demands;
- economic unity: occasionally economic developments encouraged nationalist aspirations.
- a common ethnic background: many held the view that there was something distinctive, almost tribal, about different nations – beliefs, attitudes, culture, ties of blood and kinship hallowed by time and close community.

Nationalists stressed or developed those elements which best established the separate identity of their nation. In general their hope was for some kind of political recognition of their nation; ultimately this meant the creation of an independent nation state. Over much of Europe the first task of nationalists was to develop a sense of national identity amongst a significantly powerful or influential portion of the nation. The most fruitful soil was amongst those elements of the existing élites or the educated and literate who were not committed to maintaining existing political arrangements. Only when there was significant national awareness could nationalists hope to mobilise support to achieve nationalist aims.

The desire for national recognition, for some kind of political autonomy or a nation state, placed nationalism firmly on the side of those opposed to the status quo (such as the educated middle classes) and to the system of dynastic, absolutist states and empires, supported by aristocratic landowners and the church. The idea of the nation and the nation state provided an alternative vision of political organisation which was attractive to both moderate liberals and radicals alike. Whilst liberals tended to envisage a monarchy limited by a constitution which would give property owners a share of political power (as in Britain), radicals tended to want a more democratic system which would give all men the vote. Both opposed absolute monarchy and both could justify their claims for rights, reforms and political power (as the French had done in 1789) as the legitimate demands of the nation. Nationalism, then, could provide the ideological common ground which could allow both liberals and radicals to work together against the existing order.

2 The Growth of Nationalist Movements

> **KEY ISSUE** To what extent and why did nationalist movements develop in this period?

a) Nationalism and Religion: Ireland and Russia

The development of Irish nationalism in the nineteenth century was closely bound up with religion. Wolfe Tone, the protestant Irish leader of the 1790s, had referred to the Catholics in Ireland as the 'Irish, properly so-called',[1] but it was Daniel O'Connell, 'the Liberator', who created a nationalist mass movement which used Catholicism as its cement. When Ireland had lost its limited degree of semi-independence with the Act of Union in 1800, Catholic Irishmen lost their political influence by being debarred from the franchise and political office. O'Connell's Catholic Association (1823) took up the issue of Catholic representation and harnessed Irish Catholic opinion so successfully that the British government was reluctantly compelled to accept Catholic Emancipation (allowing Catholic MPs and Catholic voters) in 1829 rather than risk mass unrest. The Catholic nature of Irish nationalism was reinforced by the economic dominance of the largely Protestant Anglo-Irish landlords who owned the land from which the Catholic peasantry scratched a living. What is significant is that O'Connell had used religion to create a popular mass movement, and thenceforward the character of Irish nationalism was inextricably linked to Catholicism.

In Russia, too, nationalism went hand in hand with religion, but Russian nationalism was state-sponsored, designed to bolster the autocratic regime of the Tsar. Russian identity, already demonstrated in resistance to Napoleon, gained strength from the Orthodox Church which supported, and was defended by, the Tsar. Religion then could help bind the people in loyalty to the Tsar and provide a common Russian identity which could be used by the Tsarist regime to strengthen the sense of Russian separateness and defend it against revolutionary ideas from the west. Nicholas I (1825–55), using the slogan 'Orthodoxy, Autocracy, Nationality', adopted the policy of 'official nationality' to help bind his subjects together. Propounded by priests, journalists, courtiers and academics, official nationality identified being Russian with the Orthodox Church, acceptance of the absolute rule of the Tsar, and 'Russianness' (nationality). Russians were different because of their history and language; they had a different temperament, different beliefs, a different outlook from other people. Writers like Pushkin promoted the Russian language and wrote about Russian heroes like Boris Godunov and Peter the Great. To minimise internal dissent from minorities in the Russian Empire, some argued for a policy of 'Russification' of non-Russian parts of the Russian empire, like the Baltic states and Poland. Others, whilst maintaining the distinctiveness of Russians, pointed to the common background of all Slav peoples and promoted Russia as the protector of Slavs outside Russia.

b) Nationalism and Culture, Language and History: The Austrian Empire

The Austrian Empire's unity derived from the fact that all within it owed allegiance to the Habsburg monarchy. Nationalism, of course, posed a huge threat to this 'worm-eaten house' which included within its boundaries Germans, Hungarians, Poles, Czechs, Slovaks, Ruthenes, Slovenes, Serbs, Croats, Rumanians and Italians. The Austrian Chancellor Metternich, fearing that political nationalism would destroy the Empire, sought to stifle any possible revolutionary threat by a combination of strict censorship, the use of spies and informers, and the monitoring of mail.

However, Metternich also promoted cultural differences within the Empire as part of the traditional Habsburg policy of divide and rule, exploiting mutual jealousies and rivalries to prevent concerted action against Vienna. This policy had two strands, both of which unintentionally contributed to the growth of political nationalism. The first was to respect local institutions, such as provincial 'diets' (assemblies). The most important of these was that of Hungary which, although its powers were strictly limited, provided a forum for discussing political ideas, albeit by a limited (largely noble) group of people. The second was to encourage the development of regional languages, culture and history. So, for instance, Vienna financed the nationalist Ljudevit Gaj in his development of Croat language and culture. As Metternich said himself in the wake of the revolutions of 1830, such policies would prevent successful revolutionary contagion in the Austrian Empire: 'If the Hungarian revolts ... we should immediately set the Bohemian against him, for they hate each other, and after him the Pole, or the German, or the Italian.'[2]

In the longer term, however, Metternich's policy provided encouragement for nationalists seeking to develop a national consciousness amongst the people and in this period the foundations of Czech, Hungarian, Croat, Rumanian and other national identities were laid.

The most important nationalist movement was in Hungary. At first the moderate liberal aristocrat Széchényi campaigned for the revival of Magyar language and culture. Later the more influential Lajos Kossuth rallied the gentry and lesser nobility, based in Hungary and excluded from high office, to the nationalist cause and sought political independence. His Magyar (Hungarian) language newspaper, *Pesti Hirlap*, helped spread the message. The first major breakthrough was the establishment of Magyar as the official language of the Hungarian Diet in the 1840s. Kossuth's programme was more radical than Széchényi's; he was hoping to unite all social classes in support of a nation state based on the lands of the Crown of St Stephen, the historic Hungarian kingdom. He called for basic civil rights for all, free public education and the abolition of serfdom. But this attractive programme failed to win the support of all within the lands of St Stephen partly because much of the population was not Magyar, but Romanian, Serb, Croat or Slovak. Whilst Hungarian nationalists were seeking to establish their own language, culture and political independence from Vienna, they were blind to the linguistic, cultural and political aspirations of other sectors of the population. They assumed that all would accept Hungarian nationality.

This conflict of nationalities within a geographical area was also seen in Bohemia where developing Czech nationalism clashed with German. The nationalist academic Palacky set up the 'Czech Mother' publishing house to promote Czech culture and develop the Czech language. In the 1830s he published a Czech national history (written in terms of conflict with the Germans). Elsewhere the first Rumanian textbooks appeared in the 1830s and the *Croatian Gazette* appeared in 1835.

c) Nationalism and Culture, Economics and Liberalism: The German Confederation

i) Obstacles

The first obstacle facing German nationalists was the German Confederation set up in 1815. This loose association of 39 states and municipalities, presided over by Austria, was determined to maintain the independence of its member states.

The Confederation was determined to repress any manifestations of liberal or nationalist activity. After a liberal nationalist student festival at Wartburg in 1817, Metternich won the Confederation's agreement to the Karlsbad Decrees (1819), which imposed strict censorship and supervision of universities. These measures effectively stifled the nationalist movement for a decade. Nationalist and liberal activity revived in the wake of the French Revolution of 1830 (which overthrew the Bourbon dynasty). In 1832 at Hambach, an 'All Germany Festival' brought together some 25,000 nationalist burghers, artisans, students and peasants. It was, according to Theodor Heuss, 'the first political popular assembly in the history of modern Germany'.[3] There was the same flag-waving and speech-making as at Wartburg in 1817, but there was a more radical edge to the demands for a united Germany. Yet, as with Wartburg, the reaction of the Confederation was repression and German nationalism was pushed underground once more.

ii) Culture and History
The emphasis on the uniqueness of German culture and history was a strong theme in the development of German nationalism. In this period academics researched German history, especially Medieval history, and the deeds of great German rulers like Frederick Barbarossa. They also investigated folklore. The studies of the Grimm brothers were based on the belief that folk tales were the source of inherited national wisdom and part of the history of the *Volk*. These expressions of Germany's cultural heritage were bought and read by an ever-growing reading public. Adult literacy in Germany in the first half of the nineteenth century has been estimated as high as three quarters of the population, about the highest in Europe.[4] This widespread sense of shared culture helps to explain the emotional appeal of Germany and the 'Fatherland' that roused mass support in the Rhine Crisis of 1840 (see page 40).

iii) Economics
Perhaps more than anywhere else, economic developments were important in promoting the national idea. There were three significant factors: the creation of a Customs Union (or *Zollverein*) covering much of the Confederation; the beginnings of significant industrialisation; and the growth in communications – roads, canals and railways.

The extension of the Prussian Customs Union of 1818 into the *Zollverein* in 1834 created economic interdependence and co-operation between an increasing number of German states under Prussian leadership, by the 1840s most major German states had joined. German nationalists were quick to grasp its potential political implications. The poet Fallersleben, for example, wrote of the *Zollverein* as 'a bond around the German fatherland, and this bond has done much more than the Confederation to bind our hearts together.'[5]

Industrialisation began to take off in the 1840s, with German states producing their own locomotives, rolling stock and rails. The growth of industry and commerce meant the growth also of a commercial and industrial middle class many of whose members espoused the ideas of free trade and sought a national political structure which would promote their concerns.

In the period after 1815 there was a massive expansion in road and canal building. The first German railway was begun in 1835 and by1846 there were over 2,000 km of track. Economists, like Freidrich List, who advocated a united Germany, viewed the development of railways as 'the firm girdle around the loins of Germany, binding her limbs together into a forceful and powerful body'.[6] So this revolution in communications, alongside the developments of the electric telegraph and the expansion of popular journalism, encouraged a sense of German unity.

In many respects the various economic developments were strongest in Prussian lands (especially in the Rhineland acquired in 1815), and certainly Prussian dominance of the *Zollverein* lent economic weight to Prussian pretensions to political supremacy in Germany. Many German nationalists in 1848 were to turn to Prussia as the potential leader of a German nation state.

iv) Liberalism

After 1815 many Germans who advocated a united Germany also supported liberalism (i.e. they wanted some kind of constitutional government). It was the liberal nationalist agenda that came to dominate the nationalist movement in Germany in the 1840s. The combination of liberals' albeit limited local success, economic developments such as the Zollverein, and the Rhine and Schleswig crises of the 1840s (see below) convinced most liberals that only in a united Germany could liberal aspirations be achieved. However, liberals were not united in their aims. Moderates envisaged, for example, a federation of liberal states under a constitutional monarch, whilst radicals pressed for the idea of a German democratic republic.

v) The emotional appeal of 'the Fatherland' – the Rhine Crisis

It was the Rhine Crisis of 1840 that was finally to put German nationalism to the forefront of political discussion. In France, the appointment of Thiers as prime minister seemed to point to a more aggressive French foreign policy after the passivity of the 1830s. This and the French press's demands for the reconquest of France's 'natural frontier' to the east – the Rhine – aroused fear and nationalist indignation in Germany. The popular German press put its weight behind the upsurge in national feeling, publishing nationalist songs such as Becher's 'They shall not have it, Our German Rhine . . .' which proved so popular that the composer Schumann put it to music. Although the Rhine Crisis was short-lived, the wave of popular nationalism could not be ignored. German rulers responded by relaxing restrictions on 'German' organisations. There was a revival of nationalist clubs and, in 1845, the first German Choral Festival. Liberals, in particular, espoused more fully the idea of a united Germany as the means to achieve their aims.

The emotional appeal of 'the Fatherland' was reinforced when the Schleswig-Holstein issue arose in 1846. The apparent ambitions of the Danes to annex German-populated Schleswig aroused a second wave of nationalist feeling. As in 1840 the crisis died away, but it was to return again in 1848.

vi) Conclusion

By the 1840s, therefore, there was an established and growing movement for national unity within the German Confederation. The songs, the journalism and the 'national' societies indicated a growing nationalism that could provide the ideological cement to bind the various pressures for reform together. By the mid-1840s there was a growing feeling that the German nation was a fact and a growing call for its political realisation in a nation state. In times of crisis the idea of Germany had widespread appeal, but the greatest commitment and support came from the educated middle class who also espoused liberalism or radicalism.

d) Nationalism, Liberalism and Radicalism: Italy

The Italian peninsula in 1815 was divided and dominated by absolute rulers. There were no constitutions. These rulers were hostile to and fearful of nationalist and liberal aspirations and sought protection under the Austrian umbrella when revolution threatened. But, as in Austria, the perception of the threat of revolution was often greater than the reality. There were revolutions in 1820–21 (in Naples and Piedmont) and in 1830 (in Modena, Parma and Bologna) (see the map on page 42), but they had little popular support and were crushed with Austrian help. Although revolutionary programmes often included ideas for a united Italy, the aims of the rebels were not primarily nationalist; rather they were liberal demands for constitutional rule. The failure of these early revolutions led Guiseppe Mazzini to propose a different approach.

Mazzini has been described as the greatest nationalist thinker of the nineteenth century,[7] and certainly he saw the goal of a united Italy as the prime aim. He believed that nations were created by God and that each individual needed to play his part in the national community. This implied a republican nation state based on universal suffrage. Hence Mazzini rejected all forms of federation. He envisaged a 'united states of Europe', in which each nation state would have its own special mission in the cause of humanity. But first nation states had to be created. In Italy, the initial task would be to create a national consciousness through education and popular participation in the struggle for independence. Poets, writers and composers could help to inspire and direct the revival of the Italian nation whilst the role of nationalist societies would be to prepare the way for a people's war of national liberation. Italians could not hope for foreign help; instead they must achieve national unity by their own efforts – *Italia fara da se* ('Italy will make herself').

Mazzini's ideas were inspiring but also idealistic and impractical. His rejection of the liberal approach which hoped to win reform from existing rulers alienated much potential middle class support. He had no strategy for winning over the peasantry; he rejected foreign help; and he rejected the possibility of leadership by an existing head of state. His attempts at starting the national war of liberation, such as the attempted invasion of Piedmont in 1833 with 200 men, bordered on the farcical.

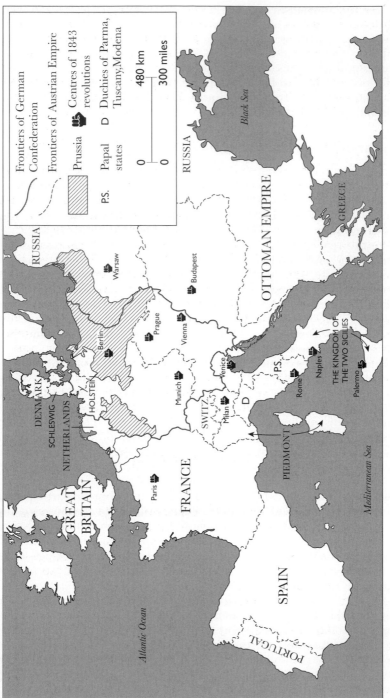

Europe 1815–1848.

But Mazzini's importance lies not so much in such actions as in the inspirational effect of his propaganda. Mazzini helped to put the idea of a united Italy firmly on the political agenda, and contributed to the growth in the 1830s and 1840s of nationalist journalism, literature and culture.

The idea of an independent Italy captured the minds of romantic writers, playwrights and composers such as Manzoni, Niccolini, Rossini and Verdi. Their writing dwelt on themes of Italian heroism against foreigners – their enthusiastic audiences clearly understood Austria to be the enemy and cheered the nationalist sentiments expressed. Other writers developed alternative visions of a united Italy. In 1843 Gioberti, in his work *Of the Moral and Civil Primacy of the Italians*, advocated the formation of an Italian federation under the leadership of the Pope, whilst in 1844 Balbo, in *Of the Aspirations of Italy*, advocated the creation of an Italian federation led by the King of Piedmont.

Other developments helped promote the idea of a united Italy. In 1839 the first of a series of congresses of Italian scientists was held in Tuscany and liberal economists began a press campaign for a customs union along the lines of the *Zollverein* in Germany. Most importantly, perhaps, moderate liberal nationalist hopes were raised with the election of the apparently liberal Pope Pius IX in 1846.

As in Germany, this period witnessed the growth, albeit limited and unsteady, of a nationalist movement. However, it remained a movement with limited appeal amongst the middle and upper classes and practically none outside the urban centres. It was also a movement divided in vision, aims and methods. In the mid-1840s, the reality was still that of a powerful Austria, of conservative rulers and mass indifference.

e) Nationalism and Outside Help: Greece, Belgium and Poland

i) Greece

The story of the Greek War of Independence (1821–1830) is complex. The revolt of the Greeks, which began in 1821, was a mass movement. As in Ireland the basis of this mass support was religion: the defence of Orthodox Christian religion against the Muslim Turks. When Archbishop Germanos declared secession from the Ottoman Empire, his call rallied the disparate elements of unrest and revolt in Greece (which drew on peasant discontent and Greek banditry). Those aspiring for a liberal nation state were confined to the small, educated middle class. Although nationalism amongst Greeks did play an important role, success in the war owed much to other factors: the weakness of the Ottoman Empire, the intervention of Britain, France and Russia and the contribution of volunteers from Western Europe and the USA. The Greeks' struggle for freedom fired the romantic imaginations of western liberals and nationalists, many of whom, like the English poet Byron, joined the fight. Such popular support also produced public pressure for British and French intervention. While fear of Russian expansion may have been the real spur to action, sympathy for liberal nationalism provided a useful justification. It was not until 1829, after defeat by Russia and under pressure from Britain and France, that the Ottoman sultan accepted Greek independence and in 1830 a Greek state with a liberal constitutional monarchy was established. In a sense, then, modern nationalism emerged the victor from a struggle which began as a defence of religion and unrest amongst the Greek peasantry.

ii) Belgium

In 1815 the territories of the former Austrian Netherlands (Belgium) were joined with those of Holland in a new Kingdom of the Netherlands. In this new creation, designed as a buffer against France, Dutch interests dominated over Belgian and the state was divided by language (Dutch, Flemish and French) and by religion (Dutch Protestants and Belgian Catholics). Conservative Catholics and liberal nationalists found common cause in the desire for separation from Holland and could point to two centuries of separate existence prior to 1815. Stimulated by the Greek example and by the July Revolution in France, revolts broke out in a number of towns in August 1830 and in October the rebels declared independence. Despite Dutch opposition, the rebellion succeeded mainly because of French and British support. Formal recognition of Belgium was to take a further eight years, but in 1839 an independent Belgium was secure.

iii) Poland

As with the Greek and Belgian revolts, the cause of Polish nationalism aroused much sympathy in western Europe, particularly in France. In contrast to the Greek situation, however, international sympathy did not result in material help and Polish nationalists were unable to mobilise mass support for their cause. When the Poles rebelled in Warsaw in 1830, they enjoyed some temporary success but were eventually crushed by the Russian army. Leading nationalists fled to Paris to lick their wounds and debate their strategy.

One problem for the Poles was that the nationalist movement was not united. Broadly, there were two groups: more moderate liberals, like Czartoryski, who placed their hopes (vainly) in French and British intervention, and more radical democratic revolutionaries who sought to overturn Russian rule by violent revolution. Neither group was strong enough or had a wide enough base of support to put their ideas into practice.

Polish nationalists were largely noble, or, as elsewhere in Europe, students, writers and academics. Nationalism had not permeated the peasantry. Attempts to identify with the Catholic peasantry against Russian Orthodox religion and to win peasant support through promises to repeal serfdom had limited success. For example, the attempted revolt in Galicia in 1846 failed when the serfs, encouraged by Austria, turned on the nobility.

f) Nationalism and the Nation State: France 1815–1848

The Revolution and the Napoleonic experience had created a common historical experience which no Frenchman could ignore. Unfortunately for the Bourbon monarchy restored in 1815, the liberals, Bonapartists and republicans could all clothe themselves in nationalist rhetoric and portray the restoration as anti-French, as representing national humiliation. The Bourbons could do little to dent that image: they returned to France in the 'baggage-train' of the Allies; Louis XVIII restored the white Bourbon flag in place of the tricolour; and Charles X was crowned in 1824 using pre-Revolutionary ceremonial which seemed to deny the idea of the sovereign nation. This was one reason why the French revolted in 1830.

After the Bourbons were overthrown in 1830, there was a definite attempt to make French nationality a reality. A standard national language and a shared national history began to be taught through the education system and the army. The attempt to spread the national idea was imbued with a sense of French greatness. France was portrayed as the guiding spirit of the modern age because they were a national community based on *liberté, égalité* and *fraternité*. In the 1830s and 1840s numerous histories of France and the Revolution by prominent journalists, historians and politicians were published and avidly read by the literate public. The monarchy, too, sought to exploit the French glories of Napoleon's rule by having the Emperor's remains brought back to France in 1840, and popular theatre, Vaudeville, created the aggressively nationalist, ex-Napoleonic soldier, Jean Chauvin (hence Chauvinism). By these means, the mass of the people of France were encouraged to see themselves as one nation with a distinctive national identity.

g) Assessment

By the 1840s, nationalist movements were growing all over Europe. Twice nationalist movements had been successful in creating nation states – Greece and Belgium. Elsewhere nationalist movements had begun to grow, but their support seemed limited to particular groups – either noble/gentry (as in the case of the Poles and the Magyars) or the educated middle classes. These were often small, if growing – even in France there were only an estimated 70,000 children in secondary schools in the 1840s.[8] In seeking to spread national consciousness, nationalists sought to develop national languages, histories and cultures to emphasise the nation's distinctiveness, but again these were only just beginning to develop in many areas before the 1840s. Nationalism seemed strongest where these were already developed and where there was some obvious historical basis to nationalist claims (amongst the Germans with the Holy Roman Empire, the Hungarians with the lands of the Crown of St Stephen, and the Poles with the Polish kingdom before 1772, for instance). Finally, nationalism could only achieve a mass following in this period where it was associated with a distinctive religious confession as in Greece.

3 Nationalism and the 1848 Revolutions

> **KEY ISSUE** What was the role of nationalism in the 1848 revolutions and in their failure?

In 1848 revolutions broke out all across Europe (see the map on page 42). Of the major powers only Britain and Russia avoided major disturbance. Historians tend to explain the outbreak of these revolutions in terms of a combination of long- and short-term causes both of which had a socio-economic and a political element. The strains and stresses caused by long-term population growth, urbanisation and a changing economy surfaced in the short-term agricultural crisis caused by Europe-wide bad harvests and potato blight alongside a financial and industrial crisis caused by over-production. Hunger, high food prices and unemployment coincided with growing demands for liberal and nationalist reforms and created politicised unrest in major towns and cities. Although unrest had begun as early as 1846 in Galicia, the real stimulus came with the revolution in France which toppled Louis Philippe in February 1848. In Metternich's view, France sneezed and the rest of Europe caught a cold. Liberal and nationalist revolts broke out everywhere. In central Europe the most significant event was the fall of Metternich, conservatism's policeman. A crisis of confidence amongst the monarchs of Europe led one after the other to give way to the demands of nationalists, radicals and liberals.

The exact role of nationalism in this 'springtime of the peoples', as contemporaries in Germany described it, is difficult to establish. The desire to create a nation state was intimately entwined with the desire for either moderate constitutional government which would give political rights to the middle classes, or for the more radical solution of full democracy and the creation of republics. Even where liberals and radicals gave some priority to the creation of a nation state there was no clear sense of the extent of that state. The situation was further complicated by the number of different nationalities which had begun to identify themselves in cultural, linguistic and ethnic terms in the first half of the nineteenth century. These different nationalities did not reside in neatly separated geographical areas. We have already seen, for instance, how Hungarian nationalists determined their hoped-for nation state in terms of the historic lands of the crown of St Stephen, which included Rumanian Transylvania and contained a range of other aspiring national groups.

What is clear, though, is that nationalism formed part of the politics of opposition in central and eastern Europe. Many nationalists, like liberals and radicals, were critical of existing dynastic, conservative and absolute regimes and sought change. In the multi-national empire of Austria and in the multi-state geographical areas of Germany and Italy, the idea of the nation state provided a powerful alternative in which liberal or democratic/republican aims could be achieved. The sovereignty of the people, as the French had already defined it, was best expressed as the sovereignty of the nation. Nationalism, then, proved a potent vehicle for opposition to existing regimes.

a) France – The Hope of Nationalists

In February 1848 the French monarchy was overthrown and a republic declared. There followed a domino effect across central Europe as rulers gave way and granted constitutions to their peoples. It was not just the fear engendered by the toppling of the monarchy in France but the apparent attitude of France to nationalists elsewhere that led rulers to grant concessions. Lamartine, speaking for the new French republic, declared on 4 March: 'The treaties of 1815 no longer exist in the eyes of the French republic'. He went on to add the France would protect 'legitimate movements for the growth of people's nationalities'.[9] It seemed that existing rulers might face not just the unrest of their own subjects but the might of a revived France as well. In fact Lamartine's words did not lead to action as simultaneously he was busy trying to reassure other rulers of French passivity, claiming that 'public impatience [had to] be fed by high-sounding phrases'.[10] What is more, conservatives came to dominate the new Republic after the crushing of radicals in June. But initially the apparent support of France gave encouragement to nationalists everywhere and caused fear in the palaces of kings.

b) Austrian Empire – The Worm-Eaten House that Failed to Collapse

The shock news of Louis Philippe's overthrow encouraged nationalist liberals and radicals in the Austrian Empire. On 3 March Lajos Kossuth made a violent speech in the Hungarian Diet condemning the 'Viennese system' whose 'pestilential breath steals over us ... paralyses our nerves and deadens our national spirit'.[11] Meanwhile, unrest exploded in Vienna itself. Metternich was sacrificed and only avoided the anger of the crowd by escaping in a laundry van. Between Metternich's dismissal and May 1848 events moved rapidly and the revolutionaries carried all before them in all parts of the Empire.

In Vienna the Emperor agreed to the drawing up of a national constitution. He also allowed the creation of a Hungarian government responsible solely to its Diet, which, in the April Laws, declared Hungary virtually independent. In Prague nationalists demanded autonomy for Bohemia. In Italy, both Milan and Venice had risen in revolt and Piedmont had set itself up as the leader in a war of 'national liberation'. By May 1848 the Poles in Galicia were demanding the creation of an independent Poland and the Slav nationalities' representatives were assembling in a Slav Congress in Prague. Everywhere established authority gave way to nationalist, liberal and radical pressure. But this was not 1789 writ large. Whilst concessions were made in the hysteria of revolutionary fervour, the Austrian Emperor remained on his throne and his armies remained loyal. The paralysis of Imperial authority was to be temporary.

The success of nationalists proved illusory. Ironically, the very nationalism which had inspired the revolutions was also to destroy their chances of success. On top of divisions between liberals and radicals, the inherent loyalty of the armed forces and the indifference of the peasantry, came divisions between the various nationalities. Metternich's policy of encouraging cultural nationalism in the period before 1848 was to bear fruit. In Galicia the Emperor was able to play on the antipathy between the Polish majority and the Ruthenian minority. In Bohemia, the hostility between Germans and Czechs enabled the army to restore imperial authority in Prague in the summer of 1848. And against Hungary the imperial government was able to play on the fears of the Slav nationalities, particularly the Croats, to undermine the new Hungarian state: indeed the Croats were to fight the Hungarians.

c) Germany – Speeches and Majority Decisions

As the Prussian monarchy along with others in the Confederation gave way to liberal and nationalist demands in March 1848, the hopes of German nationalists seemed about to be realised. In May the Frankfurt Parliament, with elected representatives from across Germany, began its attempt to create a constitution for a new united Germany. Radicals wanted a democratic, republican Germany. The moderate majority, however, envisaged a federal constitution, headed by a monarch and made in agreement with the existing princes. Both approaches begged the question of the exact territorial extent of the new Germany and the attitude to be taken to other nationalities which might or might not be included in the new state. Such questions were to arouse vigorous and prolonged debate and in the end helped to destroy the national project started so hopefully in March. The Parliament was also the focus of social and economic demands from workers and peasants which aroused fears of social revolution and mob rule.

Debate took precedence over action, and despite setting up a provisional government, little was done to make it effective. The Parliament had no army. The Schleswig-Holstein question revealed Frankfurt's weakness. Whilst Frankfurt supported German nationalist claims in Schleswig, it could do nothing without the Prussian army, and Prussia made peace rather than offend Britain and Russia by war with Denmark.

Thwarted over Schleswig, the parliament turned to the territorial arrangements for the new Germany. Many Prussian representatives favoured a *kleindeutsch* (little German) solution which simply excluded Austrian lands. However, the majority of representatives and especially Catholic southern deputies preferred the alternative *grossdeutsch* (big German) solution which would include Austrian lands which were inside the German Confederation as well as Prussian lands outside it. The *grossdeutsch* solution, of course, offended the nationalist aspirations of the Danes in Schleswig, the Poles in Prussian Posen and the Czechs in Austrian Bohemia. In any case, the splitting of the Austrian Empire was always going to be unacceptable to Vienna, which had by now recovered much of its authority in its Empire and northern Italy. Reluctantly, therefore, the Frankfurt Parliament was persuaded to take up the *kleindeutsch* solution.

Given the majority of moderate liberals in the parliament, it is not surprising that the republican route was rejected in favour of a federation of existing states and princes. The King of Prussia was the obvious choice to lead this *kleindeutsch* Germany. However, Frederick William IV rejected the offer. He had already reasserted his authority in Prussia and was not about to allow himself to become the constitutional puppet of an elected parliament – or, as he put it, 'the serf of the revolution'. Any offer of the German crown had to come from his fellow princes, not the people.

His rejection of the crown in April 1849 was followed by repeal of constitutions in other German states and the recall of representatives from Frankfurt. The forces of reaction were in full spate and the Frankfurt Parliament rapidly became untenable. The attempt to unify Germany by debate had failed.

d) Italy – Italy Fails to 'Make Herself'

As in Germany, Italian nationalists agreed on very little. Few nationalists were nationalists first; their nationalist vision was shaped by their liberalism or republicanism. Amongst republicans there was division between federal republicans, like Manin in Venice, and the Mazzinians, who sought the ideal of a unitary democratic state;

amongst liberals there was a division between those who, following Gioberti, looked for papal leadership and those like Balbo who looked to Piedmont.

But, as elsewhere, in the spring of 1848, the forces for change seemed to carry all before them. Charles Albert in Piedmont granted a constitution, as did the pope and the King of Naples. There was revolution in Venice, Milan and the central Italian duchies. Here was the opportunity to oust Austria from the peninsula and achieve political change. Milan appealed to Charles Albert of Piedmont to lead a war of liberation against a weakened Austria, but 'King Wobble' hesitated. Charles Albert was neither a liberal nor a nationalist. On the other hand, he might be able to exploit the level of unrest and nationalist feeling to secure Piedmontese interests; so, in the end, he launched a war of liberation, declaring '*Italia fara da sé*' – 'Italy will make herself'. Other Italian states, liberal nationalists and even Mazzini gave Charles Albert their support. But Charles Albert was defeated at Custozza in July. Meanwhile the pope and the King of Naples had withdrawn their support. A renewed attempt was made the following March but once more the Piedmontese were crushed (this time at Novara) and Austrian forces advanced to restore control in Lombardy and the central Italian duchies.

With that defeat and the subsequent surrenders of Rome and Venice, the hopes of liberals, radicals and nationalists were finally extinguished. Everywhere, with the significant exception of the Piedmontese *statuto*, constitutions were abolished and the old order returned in triumph. Charles Albert's and Mazzini's boast that Italy would make itself had proved a vain hope. Nationalism was not strong enough, nationalists were not united enough, revolutionaries commanded insufficient support (especially amongst the peasantry), liberals and radicals were too divided and Piedmont too weak to secure success in 1848–49.

4 Conclusions: The Significance of 1815–1848

> **KEY ISSUE** How significant was the growth of nationalism up to 1848?

The 'springtime of the peoples' did not lead to a summer of nation states. By the end of 1849 it seemed reaction and conservatism had triumphed everywhere. No single new nation state had emerged, and even the Croats who had helped the Austrian Emperor restore his authority were not rewarded with concessions to national feeling. It appeared that the nationalist threat to the established order was dead. But this is only half the truth because by 1848 many people across the length and breadth of Europe had begun to define themselves in terms of their nationality, to read and speak in their own national language and to seek political expression of their nationality. By 1848 it begins to make sense to refer to Danes and Belgians, Irish and Germans, Croats and Czechs, Italians and Greeks. Nations were identifying their own distinctive cultures and histories and developing their own written languages. A crucial first political demand of nationalists was official recognition of their national language. The period 1815–1848 witnessed the 'awakening' of national consciousness across a wide swathe of Europe. But it was a consciousness which was confined to limited sectors of the population and failed in most areas to penetrate the masses.

The varied nature of nationalist movements and the universal failure of 1848 have stimulated debate on a number of issues:

- How strong was nationalism in this period? Traditional histories of Italy, for instance, have tended to emphasise its importance in the story of Italian Unification, but revisionist studies have minimised its impact. Bismarckian interpretations of German unification have also tended to minimise nationalism's importance before 1848, whilst other interpretations have argued that German nationalism had achieved widespread support by the 1840s.
- Why had nationalism generally failed to penetrate the masses by 1848? One argument is that the spread of nationalism depended on literacy, which effectively confined its impact to the educated classes. Another is that national identity had to be invented. Crucially, until there was a national history, a national culture and a national language, nationalism could not develop. For Czechs, Croats and Romanians, for instance, these only began to be developed in this period. On the other hand there were mass nationalist movements in Ireland and Greece where literacy was low, but a strong religious identity was high.
- Why were Greeks and Belgians able to establish nation states in this period? Was it due to the strength of nationalist support or are other factors crucial? Certainly success came partly as a result of foreign support. Success also came when the powers being challenged (the Ottoman Empire and the Netherlands respectively) were relatively weak compared with their opponents.
- Why did the revolutions of 1848 fail to achieve nation states? Some have pointed to the narrow basis of support for nationalism in 1848. Was 1848, as Sir Lewis Namier described it, merely a 'revolt of the intellectuals'? Others have pointed to the internal divisions amongst nationalists. For example, between *kleindeutsch* and *grossdeutsch* German nationalists, or rivalries between German and Czech, Hungarian and Croat, or between federalists and republicans, or between reformers and revolutionaries. Other explanations focus on the resilience of the rulers and the loyalty of their armies, or the lack of help from France or the indifference of the masses.
- Was nationalism simply a movement of opposition? Two examples examined in this chapter would suggest otherwise – France and

Russia. Here, where the nation state was already in existence, national identity could be encouraged by the state to bolster support for the regime – be it liberal or autocratic.

Whilst it is true that no nation state was successfully created in 1848, the revolutions of that year had shaken the confidence of existing regimes. The issue of national identity and the creation of nation states was now firmly on the political agenda. National consciousness had been aroused and politics would in future operate in the context of national aspirations. Within 25 years the aspirations of at least the moderate nationalists of 1848 would be realised in Italy, Germany and Hungary.

References

1 As quoted in D.G. Boyce, *Nationalism in Ireland*, 3rd edition (Routledge, 1995), p. 127.
2 As quoted in E. Wilmot, *The Great Powers 1814–1914* (Nelson, 1992), p. 52.
3 Quoted in H. Schulze, *The course of German Nationalism* (Cambridge, 1991), p. 62.
4 Figure taken from J. Sperber, *The European Revolutions, 1848–51* (Cambridge, 1994), p. 32.
5 Quoted in W. Carr, *A History of Germany, 1815–1990*, 4th Edition (Edward Arnold, 1991), p. 24.
6 Ibid, p. 28.
7 M. Broers, *Europe after Napoleon* (Macmillan, 1996), p. 98.
8 Figure quoted in E.J. Hobsbawm, *The Age of Revolution 1789–1848* (Abacus, 1977), p. 167.
9 As quoted in A. Cassels, *Ideology & International Relations in the Modern World* (Routledge, 1996), p. 58.
10 As quoted in R. Tombs, *France 1814–1914* (Longman, 1996), p. 379.
11 As quoted in L.W. Cowie and R. Wolfson, *Years of Nationalism: European History 1815–90* (Edward Arnold, 1985), p 155.

Summary Diagram

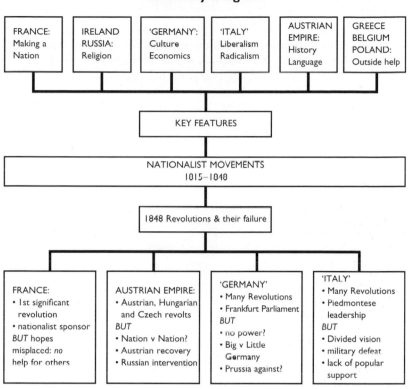

Answering stepped questions on Chapter 3

AS questions may include some stimulus material followed by two or three structured questions. Look carefully at the cartoon below, and consider the following questions on events in Europe in 1848–9:

a) Identify the figures labelled A and B. Explain their role in the events of 1848–49 (*10 marks*)

b) Explain the main reasons why the 1848 revolutions in the Austrian Empire (excluding northern Italy) were unsuccessful. (*20 marks*)

c) How similar were the reasons for the failure of attempts to create a united state in Germany and Italy in 1848–49? (*30 marks*)

A cartoon of 1849 showing French, Prussian and Habsburg forces clearing the Continent of nationalists and liberal revolutionaries. Refugees seek shelter in Switzerland or across the Atlantic in the USA.

Hints and advice:

a) is relatively straightforward, requiring a demonstration of basic knowledge and understanding of the role of these two in shaping events in 1848-49. (Figure A is Louis Napoleon, figure B is Frederick William of Prussia.) Note, however, that there are only 10 marks available, so the account should not be exhaustive but should identify the key events.

b) is a direct question which requires you to identify the key reasons for the defeat of revolutions in Vienna, Prague, and Hungary. The cartoon indicates one possible reason – the role of Austrian armed forces. You should explain this and other relevant factors giving accurate evidence to support your points. Try to differentiate between major and minor factors and to show links between them.

c) requires comparison of reasons. Be careful to identify and support not only similarities but also differences and to come to a conclusion about to what extent the reasons were similar.

Answering essay questions on Chapter 3

Essay questions may be set which seek to examine the role and development of nationalism within one state or area, or may focus on the role of nationalism in causing the 1848 revolutions. Consider the following titles:

1. How great a threat did nationalist movements pose to the Austrian Empire in the period 1815-48?
2. How important was nationalism in the 1848 Revolutions?
3. Why did national movements have so little success in the period 1815–48?

Thinking about the question set is the key to developing a good answer. This is important because it is easy to miss the point of what is being asked and produce an answer of limited or marginal relevance. Each question normally has three elements: i) an indication of the relevant area of knowledge; ii) a specific focus, or theme; and iii) an instruction. Consider question 1: Here the content has two elements 'nationalist movements' and the nature of the 'Austrian Empire'. The focus is the 'threat' the movements 'posed' to the Empire and the instruction is 'How great ...?' The instruction and the focus give you an indication of the type of answer you need to give. 'How?' questions like this require *evaluation* – you will need to come to a *judgement* about the *degree* of threat as well as identifying the *type* of threat posed. Simply put, did nationalist movements pose a minor or a major threat? Or were particular movements, such as the Hungarian, of far greater significance than, say, the Rumanian? Did some nationalist movements, like the Croats, support the Empire?

Question 2: This looks deceptively straightforward – the content is the 1848 Revolutions, the focus is nationalism and the instruction is

'How important ...?' But consider the content: there are a large number of revolutions in 1848 – the examiner will be expecting you to draw examples from a range; and does the question focus simply on the course of the revolutions or on the causes, too? It is another 'How?' question, so clearly an *evaluation* is required and not simply a description of nationalism in the revolutions. Think about the following questions: Was nationalism a major or a minor cause of the revolutions? Does the answer depend on the area considered (more important in Germany than in Italy?)? How far did nationalism shape the course of the revolutions? Again did this vary according to area?

Question 3: Here the content to draw upon is 'national movements ... in the period 1815–48'; the focus is 'so little success'; and the instruction is 'why ...?' 'Why?' questions require reasons, so the key is to identify a number of reasons for national movements' lack of success. However, simply identifying and writing about a number of reasons will not get you very high marks. What the question is really looking for is for you to make a judgement about the reasons, you identify. Which are the most important? Which the least? How are the reasons related to each other? How do they combine to give an answer? In addition, you need to think carefully about the way the focus is phrased – 'so little success'. The question is not simply about why national movements failed – the phrasing indicates that although there was failure there must have been success (e.g. Belgium, Greece). Can the reasons for success help explain why other movements failed?

4 Making Nation States, 1848–78

POINTS TO CONSIDER

This chapter examines the creation of nation states and in particular focuses on the role nationalism played. It also seeks to explain why national aspirations were not achieved in other areas. The key problem for you to address here is why nation states were formed for Rumanians, Italians, Germans, Bulgars and Serbs but not for Poles.

KEY DATES

1852	Declaration of the Second Empire under Napoleon III in France.
1854–56	The Crimean War.
1859	Rumania formed from Wallachia and Moldavia.
1859–61	Italy unified.
1863	Polish revolt crushed by Russia.
1866	Austro-Prussian War.
1867	Creation of the 'Dual Monarchy' of Austria-Hungary.
1870	Franco-Prussian War, overthrow of Napoleon III.
1871	Declaration of German Empire.
1878	Creation of an independent Bulgaria; independence of Serbia.

1 Introduction

KEY ISSUE What factors led to the creation of nation states in this period?

Almost everywhere the 1848 Revolutions had failed. Liberal and nationalist aspirations appeared to have been dashed; conservative Europe appeared triumphant with the old rulers and old elites once more in charge. Prussia and Piedmont retained limited constitutions that gave liberals some hope for the future, but in general the nationalist bubble appeared to have burst. However, 1848 had shaken the foundations of *Ancien Régime* Europe and the restored old order increasingly recognised the need for change if another revolutionary wave was to be avoided. What is more, after 1848 the new ruler of France, Louis Napoleon, was committed to overturning the 1815 Vienna Settlement and showed sympathy for the aspirations of nationalists across Europe. After 1848 considerations of the 'principle of nationality' were never far from the centre of political discussion.

Over the next 30 years the map of Europe was to be transformed (see the map on page 63). In 1861 a united Italian Kingdom was proclaimed, and in 1871 a united Germany, in the form of a *kleindeutsch* ('Lesser German') Empire, was announced. Elsewhere, reform of the Austrian Empire led to the creation of the Dual Monarchy of Austria-Hungary in 1867, and independent Rumanian and Bulgarian states were created in the Balkans. The hopes of nationalists in these areas were therefore more or less realised, but the creation of these nation states was not achieved solely by pressure from below or by revolution.

Whilst the contribution of a national movement could be crucial in defining the progress towards and the shape of any eventual new state, the creation of these nation states resulted from a combination of additional factors:

i)   changes in the international situation that made the re-drawing of states possible;
ii) the leadership of a powerful state which married its own ambitions to calls for national unification;
iii) once powerful states willing to make concessions to, or too weak to resist, nationalist challenges;
iv) the active involvement of one or more great powers willing to use force or the threat of force to overcome obstacles to change.

The existence of these factors helps to explain why war and diplomacy were so important in bringing the new nation states into existence. Nations failed to achieve statehood, however strong their nationalist movements were, if these factors were not present. This helps explain why Poles, Czechs, Croats, Slovaks and others all failed to achieve nationhood in this period.

2 Changes in the International Situation

> **KEY ISSUE** How did international relations develop in the 1850s and 60s?

The Crimean War (1854–56) between Russia and the alliance of Britain, France, Piedmont and the Turkish Empire broke the Holy Alliance and the European peace that had lasted since 1815. The Holy Alliance was broken because Austria took the position of armed neutrality against Russia during the war, fearing her attempt to extend her influence into the Balkans via Wallachia and Moldavia. The war also weakened both Austria and Russia and led Britain to adopt a more isolationist policy in international affairs. Finally, the 1850s and 60s saw the rise to prominence of able politicians and diplomatists in Piedmont (Cavour) and Prussia (Bismarck) who were willing to exploit the new situation to further their states' ambitions.

However, perhaps the key figure in international politics, at least before 1860, was Napoleon III.

3 Napoleon III and the 'Principle of Nationality'

> **KEY ISSUES** How committed was Napoleon III to supporting nationalist movements?

a) Napoleon's Foreign Policy Aims

Napoleon's appeal in France was manifold and, of course, linked closely with the Napoleonic legend: he was the restorer of order, the leader who stood above party and faction, the statesman who would unify the nation, the emperor who would restore French national pride and pursue '*la gloire*'. However, his accession to power was greeted with trepidation in the courts of Europe, where the spectre of Napoleon Bonaparte still loomed large. Would this new Napoleon pursue similar policies of war and conquest?

In foreign affairs, Napoleon III's policy was shaped by a variety of motives. He was, of course, affected by his view of his uncle, Napoleon Bonaparte. He wanted to overturn the Vienna settlement, secure France's natural frontiers, restore France's national pride and international prestige, and act as the patron of the 'principle of nationality'.

> March at the head of the ideas of your century, and those ideas will strengthen and sustain you; march behind them and they will drag you after them; march against them and they will overthrow you.[1]

So said Napoleon III. One such idea was 'the principle of nationality'. He wanted, as he often told Cavour, to 'do something for Italy'; he also supported the Poles and Rumanians and the creation of a German national state (so long as it was weak). However, his sympathy for nationalism was always tempered by a concern for French interests, glory and public support at home. By helping aspiring national movements, for instance, France would gain allies and satellites. As Napoleon III himself put it in 1859: 'a great nation is like a star – it cannot live without satellites'.[2]

However, the international community were deeply suspicious of this new Napoleon. Hence his first moves in foreign affairs were to try to reassure the major powers. 'The Empire means peace,' he declared. A useful soundbite, maybe, but its meaning was not clear and to foreign states it appeared a contradiction in terms.

Napoleon III's first attempt to restore French international prestige in the Crimean War was successful. This war resulted both from the French quarrel with Russia over the rights of Catholic and Orthodox Churches in Turkish-controlled Palestine and more importantly from Russian expansionist aims at the expense of the

Turkish Empire. France fought alongside Britain, Turkey and Piedmont and won. The resulting peace conference took place in Paris, and France once more appeared to be the arbiter of European affairs. As noted above, the Crimean War had important consequences for international relations, but one issue raised at the Paris Peace Conference by Cavour was the Italian question, a question in which Napoleon III had some interest.

b) 'Doing Something for Italy', 1859

The legacy of his uncle's victories in the peninsula and declaration on St Helena that he hoped to free the Italians (see page 21), coupled with his own past as an Italian nationalist conspirator, encouraged Napoleon III to think of 'doing something for Italy'. Now Austria had been isolated by her anti-Russian neutrality in the Crimean War the time to do something seemed opportune. Paradoxically what prompted the decision to take action appeared to be the attempt of a radical Italian nationalist to kill Napoleon III in January 1858. At his trial, the would-be assassin, Orsini, appealed to the Emperor: 'The present state of Europe makes you the arbiter of whether Italy is free or the slave of Austria and other foreigners.... The happiness or unhappiness of my country depends on you'.[3]

Napoleon responded to the appeal and signed the Treaty of Plombières with Piedmont (1858). Napoleon's approach to the Italian question was not, however, unambiguous support for the idea of a united peninsula. Indeed the last thing he wanted was to replace a powerful Austria in Italy with a powerful Italian state. However, a weak Italy under French influence was attractive. So Napoleon hoped not only to help Piedmont create a kingdom in north Italy at the expense of Austrian influence but also to secure France's southern natural frontier by acquiring Nice and Savoy, create a central Italian kingdom under French influence and appease Catholic opinion at home by ensuring the new Italy was a federation under the leadership of the pope. In this way support for the 'principle of nationality' could serve a range of French policy aims.

The role of the French army (see page 64) was decisive in creating a united Italy. However, the resultant Italian state was more powerful than France wanted and French influence over it was slight. Indeed, the French policy of protecting the pope in Rome ironically set the French against Italian nationalists who saw Rome as the natural capital of a united Italy. Even the eventual gain of Savoy and Nice was double-edged as it seemed to confirm other states' (including Britain's) worst fears about French expansionism. Indeed the cry of frustrated nationalist public opinion in France had been 'to the Rhine!' This purported threat had led Prussia to mobilise in 1859 and pose as the defender of Germany. In this way French policy had inadvertently encouraged German nationalists to look to Prussian leadership in a drive for a German nation state.

c) Napoleon III and the German Question

Napoleon's approach to the German question was perhaps more obviously shaped by French ambitions to secure her natural frontiers along the Rhine (in Germany) and the Scheldt (Belgium) than to support German nationalist aspirations. The break-up of the German Confederation would be another nail in the coffin of the Vienna Settlement, but, on the other hand, a strong unified Germany would threaten France. What is more, German nationalists were deeply suspicious of French ambitions. Napoleon's approach was therefore not one of direct involvement but one which sought to gain advantages from any reshaping of Germany. But France failed to win territory as a result of her neutrality in the Austro-Prussian war (1866) (see below) or in the subsequent attempt to buy Luxembourg from the Dutch (1867) as compensation for the Prussian creation of the North German Confederation. This became a source of French national humiliation and led to the desire to teach Prussian-led Germany a lesson. These feelings within influential French public opinion were to contribute directly to the outbreak of the Franco-Prussian War in July 1870 (see below). So, Napoleon III's espousal of the principle of nationality, whilst arguably sincere, was always complicated by other motives and factors which led to failure. A strong Italy and a strong Germany, however justifiable in nationalist terms, were not compatible with French national interest; but French intervention in 1859 in Italy and neutrality in the Austro-Prussian war in 1866 played their part in bringing about both states.

4 Nationalism and the Unification of Italy

> **KEY ISSUE** How important was nationalism in the unification of Italy?

The story of Italian unification is often portrayed as the result of the actions of individuals – King Victor Emmanuel of Piedmont, his prime minister Cavour, the nationalist guerrilla leader Garibaldi, and Napoleon III – and war (in 1859, 1866 and 1870–71) (see the map on page 63). However, nationalism did play a significant role.

a) How Strong was Nationalism in Italy After 1848?

The revolutions of 1848 had failed, and nationalists and liberals appeared as powerless after the failure as they had done before. The one glimmer of hope was the retention of the *statuto* – a limited constitution – in Piedmont. The lesson of 1848 appeared to be that romantic idealism, intellectual debate and a divided movement, however enthusiastic, could not succeed against the existing order unless supported by force. Many nationalists of whatever hue – republican, federal, liberal or democratic – came to realise the need for unity and power. They focused their hopes on the one 'liberal', independent and 'Italian' monarchy in the peninsula – Piedmont. For example, Gioberti renounced his idea of a papal federation, Manin, the Milanese revolutionary, gave up his dream of a federal republic, and even Garibaldi, the military hero of Mazzini's Roman Republic in 1849, saw Victor Emmanuel as the King of a united, and if possible democratic, Italy. Victor Emmanuel, for his part, could see the virtue of marrying the traditional policy of extending Piedmontese influence in Italy with the legitimising idea of nationalism. But after defeat in 1849 nationalist hopes and Piedmontese dreams of expansion seemed equally far from realisation as Austria reasserted her authority and the pope set his face against any liberal or nationalist advance.

b) Cavour and Nationalism

Camillo di Cavour had before 1848 been a moderate liberal nationalist, the editor of the newspaper which took its name from that of the movement for Italian unity – *il Risorgimento*. But he was no revolutionary and his hopes for Italian unification were tempered by his loyalty to the Piedmontese monarchy, his rejection of democracy and his sense of practical politics.

As prime minister from 1852, Cavour wanted to establish Piedmont as the unchallenged leader of Italy by encouraging her military and economic development whilst maintaining her liberal credentials. In this he was successful: military spending was increased, railways were built (over 800 km) and trade trebled in the 1850s.

However, British historians like Denis Mack Smith and Derek Beales argue that Cavour had no clear plans to achieve Italian unification and that he is best seen as someone who attempted, with great success, to exploit existing circumstances. His aim was to increase Piedmontese influence in northern Italy and this necessarily meant the removal of Austria. To achieve this he could exploit nationalist feeling but he also realised he needed foreign help and looked to France under Napoleon III as the best hope. An agreement was finally hammered out at Plombières in July 1858. Napoleon III agreed to go to war against Austria alongside Piedmont to win Lombardy and Venetia. The justification for the war would be 'the principle of nationalities'[4] which Austria opposed. Yet whether the 'principle of nationalities' was more than a convenient excuse is in doubt, especially as, when writing to Victor Emmanuel his account of Plombières, Cavour drew the following conclusion:

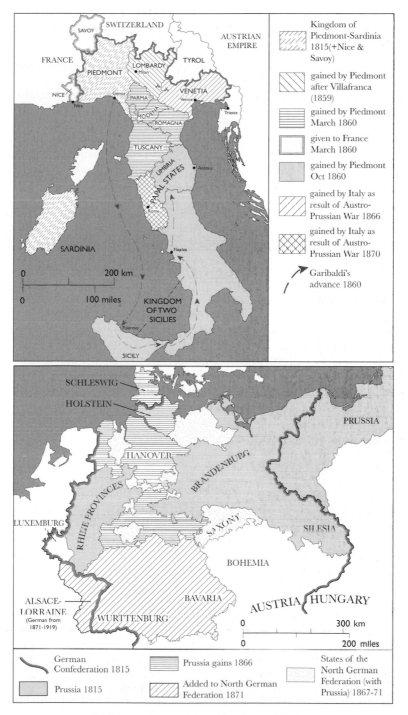

Italian and German unification, 1848–71.

> This arrangement seems to me fully acceptable. Your majesty would be legal sovereign of the richest and most powerful half of Italy, and hence would in practice dominate the whole peninsula.[5]

Arguably, then, Piedmontese expansion rather than nationalism was the real motive.

However, at another level nationalism was clearly very important in the achievement of Italian unification between 1859 and 1861. Even if expansionism was the true motive of Victor Emmanuel, he viewed nationalism as a means of winning support both in Italy and from, at least, Great Britain. When the King spoke to the Piedmontese parliament about Plombières in January 1859, he justified taking up arms in nationalist terms, referring to 'the cry of pain which comes to us from so many parts of Italy'.[6]

War broke out in the spring of 1859 and the French duly provided the bulk of the forces to fight Austria. Two bloody victories at Magenta and Solferino pushed the Austrians back, but Napoleon III then sought an armistice. He was appalled at the slaughter, feared a Prussian attack across the Rhine, and was worried by lack of support at home and the turn of events in central Italy (where existing rulers had been driven out and nationalists were demanding annexation to Piedmont). The result was the Treaty of Villafranca, which secured Lombardy (but not Venetia) for Piedmont and demanded the return of the original rulers to the central Italian duchies. In fury Cavour resigned and Piedmontese policy seemed temporarily paralysed. That Napoleon's betrayal at Villafranca did not end the process of unification was largely due to the work of nationalists in the central Italian states.

d) The Role of Nationalism

Prominent nationalist leaders had set up an Italian National Society in 1857 to organise support for Piedmontese leadership of Italy. This organisation set up committees across the peninsula and acted as a kind of link between Cavour, the moderates and more radical nationalists like Garibaldi. It produced nationalist propaganda, preaching the need for unity, Italian independence and the leadership of Victor Emmanuel. More importantly, it organised volunteers (estimated at 20,000) from across the peninsula to fight in the war of 1859 and provoked and led the revolutions in central Italy which moved the process of unification beyond the stalled start made at Villafranca. When war broke out in 1859 nationalists in Tuscany, Parma, Modena and the Romagna forced the existing rulers to flee and set up provisional governments. Elected assemblies voted for annexation to Piedmont. This persuaded Cavour, now back in office, to square Napoleon III by ceding Nice and Savoy to him in return for Piedmontese absorption of the central Italian states. These changes were legitimised by plebiscites organised by the nationalist provisional governments. Similar plebiscites were held in Nice and Savoy justifying their transfer to France. All seemed in accord with the wishes of the people. The principle of nationality appeared triumphant.

e) Garibaldi

By April 1860, then, northern Italy, apart from Venetia, had been united under Victor Emmanuel. Cavour and Piedmont would happily have stopped there – further unification would only make international intervention more likely, and was not necessarily in Piedmontese interests. However, Garibaldi thought differently.

If any figure in the Risorgimento was unequivocally an Italian nationalist it was Garibaldi; and if anyone in the *risorgimento* commanded a reputation across Italy it was he. In April 1860 he received an appeal from Sicily, where revolt had broken out against Naples. Here was a chance of another nationalist uprising that could help unite the whole of Italy. Garibaldi responded to the appeal and gathered a force of about a thousand men to go the Sicilians' aid. Cavour feared the implications of such an adventure but could not openly oppose Garibaldi without appearing to betray the nationalist cause. Neither could he openly support Garibaldi for fear of the international effects. He also distrusted Garibaldi as a democrat and ex-Mazzinian. So, without open government support, Garibaldi set sail in two old steamers with his 1,000 redshirts and some obsolete muskets. The odds seemed heavily against success as the Neapolitan army in Sicily was 25,000 strong and well-equipped, but succeed Garibaldi did.

Garibaldi's amazing success in first driving the Neapolitan army from Sicily (July) and then conquering Naples (September) threatened everything Cavour had achieved so far. Although Garibaldi fought in the name of Victor Emmanuel, he hoped for a democratic state; he also aimed to secure Rome as the Italian capital. The last might well provoke French intervention (Rome being defended by French forces), and Cavour was determined to ensure an Italy dominated by Piedmont. He therefore gambled. The Piedmontese army invaded the Papal States but skirted Rome. To get to Rome Garibaldi would now have to fight Victor Emmanuel, in whose name he purported to have been fighting. In October 1860 Garibaldi backed down and handed over his conquests. Cavour had won and in March 1861 Victor Emmanuel became the ruler of the new Kingdom of Italy.

The completion of Italian unification after 1861 had little to do with Italian nationalism but was the by-product of foreign wars. In 1866, Italy's prize for supporting Prussia in the war against Austria was Venetia (if without Istria and the Italian Tyrol), and in 1870 Italy took advantage of the withdrawal of French forces (to fight Prussia) to annex Rome. In 1870 it appeared that the nationalists had achieved their dream of a united Italy. Nationalism had been crucial in its creation, especially in securing the central Italian states and, in the person of Garibaldi, in securing the addition of the south. But it was not the Italy Mazzini or the federalists had envisaged. It was an Italy dominated by Piedmont and with a constitution which allowed only 2 per cent of the people the vote.

5 Bismarck, Nationalism and German Unification

> **KEY ISSUE** In what ways did nationalism contribute to the unification of Germany?

a) The Creation of the German Empire

In the palace of Versailles in January 1871 the German princes offered the Prussian king the title of German Emperor. This new German Empire created a united Germany without Austria; it was the *Kleindeutsch* solution mooted in 1848. But for the first time the Germans had a nation state. What is more the new state had an apparently liberal constitution with the establishment of a Reichstag elected by universal manhood suffrage. The hopes of 1848 were realised, it appeared, in 1871. But, arguably, the creation of a united Germany had little to do with nationalism and much to do with Prussian ambition and force of arms. It had been achieved on the back of three short wars and the diplomacy of Bismarck; it was not obviously the result of popular pressure and liberal nationalist persuasion.

Such an interpretation has some substance but perhaps underestimates or fails to recognise the role played by nationalism in the creation of this German (not Prussian, note) Empire. The clue to the influence of nationalism in the unification of Germany lies in something Bismarck himself said. He aimed, he believed, to travel with a divinely-ordained 'stream of time': 'By plunging my hand into it, I am merely doing my duty. I do not expect thereby to change its course.'[7]

Bismarck was not operating in a vacuum and after 1848 the question of a united Germany was firmly on the political agenda. The future of 'Germany' was the central political question in central Europe. Bismarck recognised this and once in power sought to ensure that the German question was settled in a way acceptable to Prussia – so that Germany would be unified under Prussia and without liberal control of the monarchy.

b) The Extent of German Nationalism

After the defeats of 1848–50 German nationalism was quiet in the 1850s. The idealism of 1848 gradually gave way to recognition of political realities. German nationalism revived with the outbreak of the wars of Italian Unification in 1859. The stimulus was twofold: the success of Italian nationalism and the Italian National Society encouraged emulation, and, secondly, the belligerence of France against Austria aroused patriotic feeling in Germany and provoked fears of French ambitions on the Rhine. As in 1840, the spectre of French imperialism, reinforced by her acquisition of Nice and Savoy in 1860, aroused a wave of patriotic fervour across Germany.

In September 1859 the *Nationalverein* (National Society) was formed in Hanover. It was a liberal, middle class society promoting the leadership of Prussia over a *kleindeutsch* Germany that would exclude Austria. The hope was that Prussia, like Piedmont, would take up the leadership of the German cause and, at the same time, become more liberal in outlook. But gone was the romantic idealism of 1848. Many German nationalists at the end of the 1850s recognised nothing could be achieved without power. The liberal Frobel put it starkly when he wrote in 1859 that 'the German nation is sick of principles and doctrines, literary existence and theoretical greatness. What it wants is power, power, power ...'[8] Liberal nationalists would support a Prussia which placed itself at the head of a movement for national unification. Such liberals still believed in constitutions, the rule of law and individual liberty, but they maintained that freedom could only be guaranteed if Germany was a powerful state – and only Prussia, they believed, could provide that power.

The hope placed in Prussia at the end of the 1850s did not seem totally misplaced as its king, William I, had, for example, posed as the defender of Germany against France in 1859 by mobilising the Prussian army. In Prussia itself Liberals dominated the Landtag (Parliament). But liberal hopes of Prussia seemed dashed when the Liberals in the Prussian parliament clashed with the Prussian king over the issue of Army Reform. This led to a constitutional crisis resolved only by the appointment of the conservative Bismarck as Minister President in September 1862. His solution was to ignore the parliament and press ahead with reform. Liberal hopes of Prussia creating a liberal German state therefore appeared dashed.

c) The Role of Economics

We have already seen how the *Zollverein* was helping to create a 'national' German economy, but the exact relationship between economic developments and unification is unclear. Certainly, Prussia, which dominated the *Zollverein*, continued to exclude Austria (as it did in 1865) and arguably the economic logic then supported the idea of a *kleindeutsch* Germany. But if economics pointed the way to political unification, the politicians certainly did not see it that way. Neither economic arguments nor Prussia's economic leverage were strong enough to persuade the majority of *Zollverein* member states to join Prussia's side in the war of 1866; indeed most sided with Austria.

On the other hand, the economic strength of Prussia (her economy 'took off' under the guidance of Manteuffel in the 1850s) gave her the resources she needed to challenge Austria in the 1860s. Herein lies the force of J.M. Keynes' argument that it was 'coal and iron' rather than 'blood and iron' (see below) which explains German unification.

d) Bismarck and Nationalism

A Russian diplomat who attended a dinner in London with Bismarck and Disraeli (later the British Prime Minister) in the summer of 1862 recorded these words of Bismarck allegedly spoken to Disraeli:

1   As soon as the army shall have been brought into such a condition to command respect, then I will take the first opportunity to declare war with Austria, burst asunder the German Confederation, bring the middle and smaller states into subjection and give Germany a national
5   union under the leadership of Prussia.[9]

Then on 30 September 1862 Bismarck famously declared to the Prussian Parliament:

1   Germany does not look to Prussia's liberalism, but to its power. Bavaria, Wurttemberg, Baden can indulge in liberalism, but no one will expect them to undertake Prussia's role. ... Prussia's boundaries according to the Treaty of Vienna [1815] are not favourable to a
5   healthy political life; not through speeches and majority decisions are the great questions of the day decided – that was the great mistake of 1848–49 – but by blood and iron.[10]

One interpretation of Bismarck's speech is that he was offering the Liberals the prospect of a united Germany in the hope that, in return, they would not continue to press for increased control over the government. Whether or not this interpretation of Bismarck's speech is correct, he failed to convince the Liberals. Liberal nationalists in Prussia and in the *Nationalverein* saw Bismarck not as a potential unifier of Germany but as an anti-liberal reactionary.

This seemed confirmed by Prussia's action over Schleswig-Holstein in 1864. In 1863 the Danes pushed their claim to incorporate Schleswig-Holstein more fully into the Danish kingdom. This was opposed by German nationalists who hoped that the German Confederation would intervene on behalf of the rival claimant the Duke of Augustenburg. Bismarck, however, wanted Prussia to annex Schleswig-Holstein and joined Austria in a brief war against Denmark that resulted in Prussia occupying Schleswig and Austria Holstein. The German Confederation and the nationalists were ignored.

In the Danish crisis German nationalists had shown themselves to be, according to Hagen Schulze, 'vociferous but impotent'.[11] Prussia had pursued her own policy without regard to nationalism. She was to push her own policy again in 1866 in her bid to gain Holstein and remove Austrian influence from northern Germany. Her direct challenge to Austria and call for reform of the German Confederation provoked war. However, on this occasion Bismarck appealed to German nationalists for support:

> The German Confederation for half a century has represented and promoted, not the unity, but the fragmentation of Germany. A majority of its members [states] abolished the Confederation when they decided to arm against Prussia. All that remains is the living unity of the German
> 5 nation. It is the duty of governments and peoples to find a new means of expressing this unity and one with the strength to last.
>
> Let the German people, with this high aim in mind, come forward in confidence to meet Prussia. Let it help to promote and make secure the peaceful development of our common fatherland.[12]

The appeal fell on deaf ears; nationalists still viewed Bismarck as a reactionary. Austria had the support of Saxony, Hanover, Bavaria, Hesse, Wurttemberg and Baden, and Prussia had provoked not a war of national liberation but a German civil war. Prussia won, defeating Austria's German allies and also Austria herself at Sadowa. It was this Prussian victory and the subsequent creation of the North German Confederation which won over nationalists; their opposition to Bismarck seemed to collapse overnight. Many German nationalists now recognised that there was, with Austria excluded from Germany, in terms of nationalism, if not liberalism, no irreconcilable differences between Bismarck's Prussian policy and *kleindeutsch* German nationalism. Most dropped their 'liberal' opposition to Bismarck. Bismarck had, it appeared, successfully hijacked the nationalist movement and linked it to the expansionist policy of Prussia. But Bismarck now found himself constrained by awakened nationalist pressure to continue the process of unification by bringing in the southern states.

Bismarck recognised that union with the southern states of Germany might strategically strengthen Prussia in relation to both France and Austria and began to feel that unification was inevitable in the long term, but he was unwilling to create this *kleindeutschland* on National Liberal terms. There was some popular pressure in the southern states for union with the north, especially in Wurttemberg and Baden, which were most threatened by France, but there was also considerable suspicion of Prussia. Bismarck was prepared to wait. He was further persuaded in this approach by the results of the elections in1868 to the Zollparlament (a parliament elected to discuss the policy of the *Zollverein*). There was a majority of opponents to the union of the south to the Prussian north. In 1869 Bismarck said:

> That German unity would be furthered by violent events I also hold probable. But it is quite another question to assume the mission of

bringing about a violent catastrophe and the responsibility for the
choice of timing.... That German unity is not at this moment a ripe fruit
5 is in my opinion obvious ...'[13]

Bismarck was happy with the informal influence Prussia exerted over
the southern states and perhaps feared the prospect of union with
states that were Catholic, more liberal and traditionally anti-Prussian
in temperament.

However, pressure for further action seemed to mount in early
1870. The National Liberals in the north were becoming impatient
and Bismarck feared a potential Franco-Austrian alliance. In addition,
what support there was in the southern states for union with the north
also appeared to be weakening. That is why, perhaps, Bismarck seized
the opportunity offered by support for a Prussian candidate to the
Spanish throne (vacant since 1868) to re-establish Prussian prestige,
even if it risked war with France. If war occurred it might provide
Bismarck with the opportunity to unify Germany on Prussian terms.
However, French pressure forced the withdrawal of the Prussian candidate. Yet the king rejected additional French demands that the
Prussian candidacy would not be renewed and it was this that provided Bismarck with the opportunity to provoke France. He cleverly
exploited the king's report of his meeting with the French ambassador by publishing a shrewdly edited version of events in the so-called
Ems telegram. The apparently stiff rebuff of French demands both
won nationalist support in Germany and goaded French national
opinion, already smarting from the debacle over Luxemburg in 1867.
The French sense of outrage caused Napoleon III to declare war.
France then appeared the aggressor and Prussia could once more
pose as the defender of German interests. Nationalist sentiment was
whipped up at home into an anti-French frenzy and, according to
Carr, 'a great wave of white-hot patriotic fervour swept through the
whole country including the south'.[14] The Prussian army once again
marched to defend Germany (even if – to do so – they marched into
France!).

After Prussian victory at Sedan (September 1870), popular pressure for unification grew, stirred up by the nationalist press and
encouraged by Bismarck. This added strength to Bismarck's negotiat-
ing hand with the south German states, which were now more willing
to make concessions to Bismarck's demands. Hard bargaining
ensured that a Prussian-dominated united Germany would give at
least some recognition to the southern princes; and victory in war
ensured nationalist support for the new German Empire declared in
January 1871. The constitution of the new Empire recognised to some
degree that national identity provided the legitimisation of the new
state. Its preamble referred to 'a perpetual union for the defence of
the federal territory and the laws obtaining within it, as well as for the
welfare of the German people'.[15]

Nationalism may not have played a direct role in the unification process between 1862 and 1871, but Bismarck had to take it into account and shape his ambitions for Prussia accordingly. That is one reason why, for instance, a German Empire emerged in 1871 and not simply a Greater Prussia; it was a sense of Germanness that gave it its identity. Nationalism gave Bismarck's ambitions for Prussia a sense of moral legitimacy. Moreover the German Empire was consistent with nationalist ambitions even if its constitution was not as liberal as some nationalists would have liked. Whilst there was universal suffrage, the powers of the Reichstag were limited. Ministers, for example, were not answerable to it.

6 Magyar Nationalism and the *Ausgleich* of 1867

KEY ISSUE What was the nature of the *Ausgleich* of 1867?

While the defeat of Austria in 1866 was decisive in the process of German unification it was also the final stimulus to reform of the Austrian Empire, forcing some concessions to Hungarian nationalism. The success of the Austrian Empire in reasserting its authority in 1849 had not meant the problem of nationalities had disappeared. The lid was put back on but the stew continued to simmer.

It was defeat of the Austrian army against France in 1859 and Prussia in 1866 that was to lead to reform of the Empire in 1867. Austria's defeat in northern Italy in 1859 provoked a financial and constitutional crisis that resulted in the introduction of limited constitutional government in 1860–61. However, this constitution, which retained the central control of Vienna, appeased neither nationalists nor liberals within the Empire. Most importantly, the Hungarians opposed the constitution and pressed for recognition of Hungary's claims to autonomy. The failure of the reforms renewed nationalist pressure after 1861, and in 1865 Vienna agreed to the reinstitution of the Hungarian Assembly.

Friction with Prussia over Germany in 1865 gave the Hungarian nationalists leverage that they were able to exploit when Austria was defeated at Sadowa in 1866. The result was the creation of the Dual Monarchy of Austria-Hungary in the *Ausgleich* ('compromise') of 1867. This divided the Austrian Empire into two halves: Austria (including Bohemia, Moravia, Galicia); and Hungary, comprising the historic lands of the Crown of St Stephen (which included Croatia, Transylvania and Slovenia). Both Austria and Hungary would have their own parliament with an administration responsible to it for internal matters. The official language of Austria was German; of Hungary, Magyar. Effectively the compromise ensured in Austria the supremacy of Germans (and politically the wealthy Germans as the franchise was carefully restricted), and in Hungary the supremacy of the Hungarians. So, the aspirations of Czechs, Poles, Slovenes and other national groups were ignored in Austria; those of Croats, Slovaks, Romanians and Serbs in Hungary. The *Ausgleich* was, then, an alliance against Slavs. The situation is perhaps best summed up by the cynical remark of the Hungarian Count Andrassy to an Austrian colleague: 'You look after your Slavs and we'll look after ours'.[16]

No wonder that the Czech national leader, Palacky, commented in 1865: 'We Slavs are a peaceful people but we warn you: do not sow the wind, lest you reap the whirlwind'.[17] The compromise effectively closed the door on the possibility of Palacky's federal dream of 1848, with the Habsburg ruler at the head of a federation of equal nations. At the same time it stimulated the growth of nationalism in these excluded groups, which now threatened to look to Russia for support. For example, Palacky was to lead a Slav delegation to the Ethnographic Conference in Moscow in 1867.

There were partial exceptions to the apparent German/Hungarian supremacy. Polish was the official language in Galicia and the Poles' Assembly was retained. And in 1868 Hungary made its own 'compromise' with Croatia. This granted Croatia its own assembly and its own government, using the Croat language, for internal affairs. However, the head of government was effectively appointed by Hungary. The year 1868 also saw the passage of the Nationalities Law in Hungary, which superficially seemed to acknowledge the rights of subject nationalities by allowing use of national languages at a local government and personal level. However, the law has been viewed by most historians as an instrument of Magyarisation because it insisted on Magyar at all important levels and disallowed the idea that nationality justified political independence. It certainly excluded non-Magyars from top government and administrative posts. Moreover the Hungarian government was to suppress potential sources of Slav nationalism in the 1870s. For instance, Slovak deputies were expelled from the Hungarian Assembly in 1872, Slovak secondary schools were closed in 1874 and a Slovak cultural society was suppressed in 1875. The Government declared triumphantly: 'There is no Slovak nation!'[18]

7 Great Power Diplomacy and the Creation of Romania and Bulgaria

> **KEY ISSUE** How important was nationalism in the creation of Romania and Bulgaria?

By 1850 the Turkish Empire, which like the Austrian and Russian Empires contained a number of subject national groups, had lost Algeria to the French, granted independence to Greece and regional autonomy to the provinces of Serbia, Wallachia and Moldavia (the

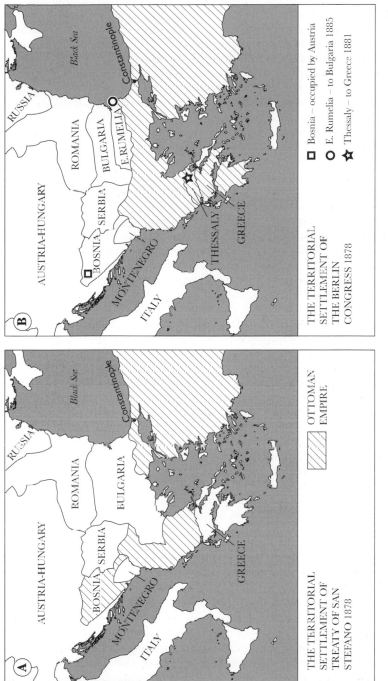

The Balkans and Central Europe 1878.

latter two provinces containing mainly Romanians); Egypt too had achieved a similar status. The Turkish Empire seemed to be in decline: this gave an opportunity not only for aspiring national groups in the Balkans to assert themselves but also for Austria and Russia to expand their influence in the region. Britain and France were also vitally concerned with this aspect of the 'Eastern Question' because of their strategic, imperial and trading interests. Generally their policy was dictated by the need to contain Russian expansionism rather than by any real interest in the problems of Balkan nationalism. That is why, for instance, they supported the Turks against Russia in the Crimean War (1853–56). Balkan nationalism was to be advanced, manipulated or retarded in the interests of the Great Powers.

Romanians occupied provinces partly in the Austrian Empire (Transylvania), partly in the Russian Empire (parts of Bessarabia) but mainly in the Turkish Empire (Moldavia and Wallachia) (see the map on page 73). It was not surprising therefore that the achievement of Romanian nationalists' aims depended heavily on the attitude, relative strength and strategic interests of these three powers and also of Britain and France, whose leaders feared Russian expansionism. One consequence of the Crimean War was that, in 1859, Wallachia, Moldavia and part of Bessarabia were united for the first time under a single government. This semi-independent Romania was seen as a more effective barrier to Russian expansionism than a weakened Turkish Empire. Romania remained nominally under Turkish rule until 1878 when the independence of the kingdom of Romania was formally recognised by the Great Powers and the Turks.

Bulgaria, too, came into existence largely as the result of the international considerations of the Great Powers. As with other Balkan national groups, Bulgar nationalism had begun to develop in the nineteenth century, partly encouraged by Russia, which hoped to increase its influence. Bulgar demands were initially quite restrained: they wanted Bulgar education and the use of the Bulgar language in churches. Under pressure from Russia, in 1870 the Turkish sultan recognised the Bulgars as a separate religious nation with its own church leader. This was seen as the first step on the road towards national independence.

When, in the mid 1870s, unrest broke out across the Balkans, from Bulgar protests against Turkish rule to Serb attempts to grab territory, Russia sought to exploit the situation. In 1877 she declared war on the Turks and forced her to make peace at San Stefano. Among other things, Turkey allowed the creation of a large Bulgarian state (under Russian influence) and the independence of Serbia, Montenegro and Romania.

This sudden extension of Russian influence alarmed the other European states fearful of a Balkans dominated by Russia. Russia was thence compelled to accept reduced terms by the Congress of Berlin

(June 1878). Whilst this affirmed the independence of Romania, Serbia and Montenegro, it reduced the size of Bulgaria. David Thomson succinctly summed up the situation in the Balkans at this time. To keep the peace in Europe, 'the nationalist aspirations of all Balkan peoples [were sacrificed] to the avarice and rivalries of the great powers'.[19] Even so by 1878 a series of independent Balkan nation states had emerged.

8 The Poles

> **KEY ISSUE** Why did the Poles fail to create a nation state in this period?

Given the climate of the late 1850s and the 1860s, one might have expected one of the strongest nationalist movements in Europe – that of the Poles – to succeed in finally achieving its aim of an independent national state. After all, the map of central Europe was being redrawn on national lines; Russia had been weakened by the Crimean War and was, under Alexander II, apparently open to reform; Austria, too, was defeated in war and facing internal problems; and Polish nationalism aroused the sympathy of the peoples of Britain and France. However, it was not to be. In fact, Poles were worse off at the end of this period than at the start.

The Poles made one major effort to overthrow their Russian masters in 1863. This came after Alexander II had attempted to conciliate them with some minor reforms, such as the acceptance of Polish as the official language, the return of Polish exiles and the establishment of new schools. Detecting weakness and disdaining co-operation with Russia, radical nationalists, whose support was drawn mainly from students and the towns, demonstrated in support of Polish independence. This renewed agitation provoked the Russian government into a rather clumsy attempt to deprive the nationalist movement of its leaders by conscripting them into the army in January 1863. The nationalists' response was to call for a general insurrection. Hopes of French aid were misplaced, Britain and Austria stood aloof and Bismarck, fearing that perhaps the revolt would spread to Prussian Posen, offered aid to Russia. So, although there was widespread unrest, the Russians were eventually able to crush the revolt.

If they were to achieve independence, the Poles, unlike other nationalist movements, would have to do so not at the expense of just one, or even two, Great Powers, but three – Russia, Austria and Prussia. Italian nationalists were able to win their independence partly because Austria was weak in 1859 and partly because they had the active support of a major power, France. A German national state was created as the result of the action of one Great Power, Prussia, against a weakened enemy in Austria and then against France. But the Poles enjoyed none of these advantages. What is more, the Polish national movement was still divided – there were the liberal aristocratic nationalists represented by the Agricultural Society, the anti-Russian Roman Catholic Church and the more radical nationalist lesser gentry and professionals. In addition, Polish nationalists had still to win over the peasantry: acquiring land was more important to most peasants than nationality or statehood.

The Tsar's response to the Polish revolt was twofold. First, Alexander II sought to bind the Polish peasantry to him by abolishing serfdom and by granting peasants title to their lands on better terms than he had given the Russian peasants in 1861. But his policy failed to turn the peasantry into a loyal conservative force. Rather the peasantry in Poland now supported their erstwhile landlords in opposing the Tsar's second policy after 1863 – Russification. Russian, not Polish, became the official language in government and education; the Polish University in Warsaw was suppressed and replaced with a Russian one; restrictions were placed on Catholic and Polish schools and on the activities of the Catholic clergy; and the kingdom of Poland was abolished. The attainment of an independent Poland once more seemed a remote possibility.

9 Conclusion: Nationalism and Making Nation States

> **KEY ISSUE** How important was nationalism in the creation of nation states?

Whilst the liberal nationalist revolutions of 1848 had failed to produce a single nation state, by the 1870s there existed a united Italian kingdom, a united German Empire, a relatively autonomous Hungary and the independent states of Serbia, Bulgaria and Romania (see the map on page 73). But none of these had come about as the direct result of liberal nationalist revolutions. The new states might have constitutions but the franchise was often limited (as in Italy) or the elected assembly had few powers (as in the German Empire). As such the new states were not the truly liberal states many nationalists had hoped for. Nor did the territorial extent of the new states encompass all of the relevant nationalities. The Kingdom of Italy did not include the Italians of Istria and the Tyrol; Austrian and Bohemian Germans were excluded from the German Empire; Romania did not include Transylvania; Serbia had ambitions on Bosnia and other lands to the south; and Greece wanted expansion at the expense of the Ottoman Empire.

1848 made the 'principle of nationality' the issue of the day in politics, but nationalists – for all their propaganda, societies, academic research and linguistic development – did not create nation states in this period. If nationalist movements were able to create states on their own then arguably the first new nation state should have been Poland. But Polish nationalists failed to win independence in 1863.

What were the ingredients for success in making nation states? Consider the following:

i)   Changes in the international situation made the re-drawing of states possible: consider the consequences of the collapse of the Holy Alliance in the 1850s, the impact of Napoleon III and the ambitions of Piedmont and Prussia;

ii) The leadership of a powerful state which married its own ambitions to calls for national unification: some have argued that rather than national unification of Germany and Italy what emerged was merely an expanded Prussia and Piedmont;

iii) Once powerful states were willing to make concessions to, or too weak to resist, nationalist challenges: arguably the relative decline of the Austrian and Ottoman Empires left them vulnerable to nationalist movements;

iv) One or more great powers willing to use force or the threat of force to overcome obstacles to change: the historian L.C.B. Seaman considered Napoleon III's contribution to be decisive in the creation of a united Italy. In the Balkans it was the intervention of the great powers which shaped the destiny of Serbs, Romanians and Bulgars.

What, then, was the role of nationalism? The following ideas bear investigation:

a)   Existing states, like Prussia and Piedmont, were able to use the legitimacy which the 'principle of nationality' conferred to justify their expansionist aims; but this principle also meant that these states' policies were also constrained by the need to resolve the national question. What emerged was not merely a Prussia expanded, for instance, but a *kleindeutsch* united Germany;

b)   Nationalists became realists after the failures of 1848–49 and worked within the potential of existing political circumstances; they were often willing to put to one side their liberal or radical aspirations and give priority to the creation of a nation state. In Italy nationalists looked to Piedmont and in Germany, certainly after 1866, to Prussia.

c)   Nationalism could have a decisive influence on the course of events. Consider, for instance, the role of the National Society in Italy in bringing the central duchies to Piedmont and the role of Garibaldi in uniting southern Italy with the north. Consider also the role of nationalism in France and Germany in bringing about war in 1870.

There are a number of other points to note about nationalism in this period. Nationalism remained a force for change where national aspirations remained thwarted – as with the Slav nationalities in Austria-Hungary or with the Poles in the Vistulaland (the old kingdom of Poland).

The loosening of links between nationalism and liberalism opened the way for the exploitation and promotion of national identity as a way of reinforcing loyalty and obedience to the state. In that sense, the potential for nationalism to act as a conservative force rather than a force for change was becoming clearer. Bismarck had learnt from his experiences as ambassador in France that universal suffrage did not necessarily unleash mob rule and radical politics, especially in rural areas: hence he was willing to include it in the Empire's constitution.

Public opinion was playing an increasingly important part in politics. National humiliation over several years and a sense of stung French pride had provoked the declaration of war on Prussia in July 1870. German nationalist pressure in the south German states had helped persuade the princes to agree to the creation of a German Empire in 1871.

Finally, it is worth noting that nationalism was still primarily an ideology of the middle and literate classes. The task facing the new nation states was to win the loyalty and active support of all their citizens.

References

1 Robert Tombs, *France 1814–1914* (Longman, 1996), p. 396.
2 Tombs, *France*, p. 403.
3 T.A. Morris, *European History 1848–1945* (Collins, 1995), p. 51.
4 Cavour to Victor Emmanuel, July 24 1858, in Derek Beales, *The Risorgimento and the Unification of Italy* (Longman, 1981), p. 157.
5 Beales, *Risorgimento*, p. 157.
6 Harry Hearder, *Italy in the Age of the Risorgimento 1790–1870* (Longman, 1983), p. 224.
7 Alan Cassels, *Ideology and International Relations in the Modern World* (Routledge, 1996), p. 76.
8 William Carr, *A history of Germany, 1815–1890* (Edward Arnold, 1991), p. 72.
9 Cassels, *Ideology & International Relations*, p. 76.
10 Carr, *Germany*, p. 78.
11 Hagen Schulze, *States, Nations and Nationalism* (Blackwell, 1996), p. 222.
12 Finlay McKichan, *Germany 1815–1939* (Oliver & Boyd, 1992), p. 54.
13 Carr, *Germany* (Edward Arnold, 1991), p. 110.
14 Ibid, p. 114.
15 Hagen Schulze, *States*, p. 224.
16 Alan Sked, *The Decline and Fall of the Habsburg Empire 1815–1918* (Longman, 1989), p. 190.
17 R. Gildea, *Barricades and Borders* (Oxford, 1996), p. 203.
18 Ibid, p. 204.
19 David Thomson, *Europe Since Napoleon* (Penguin, 1966), p. 466.

Summary Diagram

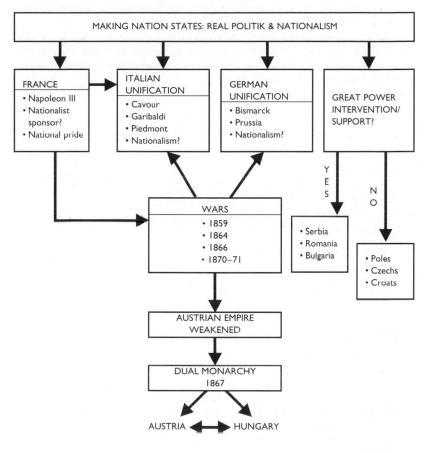

Answering source-based questions on Chapter 4

1. Bismarck and Nationalism

Read the extracts on Bismarck's attitude to nationalism on pages 68–70. Consider the following questions:

a) Explain the meaning and significance of the phrase 'blood and iron' in his speech to the Prussian parliament (page 68, line 7). (*4 marks*)

b) The report of Bismarck's conversation with Disraeli in the summer of 1862 (page 68) was published in 1887 in a book by the Russian diplomat. How useful is this source as evidence of Bismarck's intentions in Germany? (*7 marks*)

c) Look at Bismarck's proclamation to the German people of 1866 on page 69. How reliable is this source as evidence of Bismarck's attitude to German nationalism? (*7 marks*)

d) Look at Bismarck's views on German unification from 1869 on pages 69–70 and the report of the dinner conversation with Disraeli from 1862 on page 68. Compare these sources as evidence of Bismarck's ambitions for Germany. (*12 marks*)

e) Say how far, in the light of your own knowledge, all these sources support the view that Bismarck was interested in Prussian expansion rather than German unification? (*20 marks*)

Hints and Advice

Question (a) is the most straightforward type of source question. It requires two things: a reasonable explanation of the meaning of the phrase, and its relevance in this context.

Question (b) is about the strengths and limitations of this source for the purpose stated in the question. To make a judgement on these issues you will need to consider the content of the source (how much does it say of relevance? does it seem plausible?), the authorship of the source (was the author in a good position to comment knowledgeably?), the nature of the source (what sort of source is it? when was it produced?) and the context of the events reported. What would make the source more credible?

Reliability questions, like (c), are about the credibility, accuracy and typicality of evidence. You will need to examine carefully the tone and language of the source (is it sober, factual, balanced or emotive, one-sided?), the authorship (in this case it is from Bismarck so that might suggest reliability), the nature of the source (how does the fact that this is a proclamation addressed to the German people affect the credibility of the source?), and the context (do the timing and circumstances surrounding the issue of the source raise doubts?). Finally, does what is said in the source fit in with other evidence of Bismarck's views.

The key issue with (d) is that you are looking for points of comparison (points of similarity and difference) between the sources. Both these sources say something about the unification of Germany, but differ in their emphasis. Can these differences be explained? Remember also you are comparing them as evidence, which raises questions of utility and reliability, and so the questions used above will be helpful here. Try to avoid writing about one source and then the other; make comparisons throughout and come to a judgement.

Remember that, in (e), the question is asking you to test the sources in the context of what else you know about Bismarck's motives and aims. Using contextual knowledge is crucial, but you should use it to inform your evaluation of the sources. One way is to show what the sources illustrate and what they don't. But also think about the quality of the evidence. Just because three sources say one thing and only one disagrees does not necessarily make the single source wrong: it depends on the quality of the source as evidence. Try to avoid a source by source run through: rather, try to pick out themes and ideas and draw on the sources where appropriate. Also consider the sources as a set – taken together, do they provide good evidence to support the hypothesis?

Answering stepped questions on Chapter 4

AS questions on German and Italian Unification will require you to demonstrate a sound knowledge and understanding of the basic facts and the forces at work. Questions will normally be structured in two or three parts. Consider the following example:

1. **a)** Explain the contribution of the following to the unification of Italy:
     Napoleon III
     Cavour
     Garibaldi (*30 marks*)
   b) How important was nationalism in creating a united Italy between 1858 and 1861? (*30 marks*)

Hints and Advice
With regard to a) the examiner will be looking for you to demonstrate a good knowledge of the role of each individual in Italian Unification. He will also be looking for you to demonstrate some assessment of the importance of the role of that individual. For example, in relation to Napoleon III you might wish to consider the positive and negative ways in which he contributed to unification by assessing his apparent sympathy for 'Italy', his role in the Treaty of Plombières and the war of 1859, his 'betrayal' of Italy at Villafranca, his acceptance of the annexations of the central duchies in 1860 and how his willingness to defend Rome affected events in the autumn of 1860. With regard to b) the emphasis is on analysis and evaluation. As with a) you must explain the role of nationalism in Italian unification but you must also set it against other forces at work to evaluate its relative importance. Also note carefully the date restriction in the question – you are only asked about 1858-61; material included from outside this period is unlikely to be relevant.

Answering essay questions on Chapter 4

Most essay questions on Italian and German unification, the Austrian Empire and the Eastern Question require some reference to nationalism. Below are a sample of questions requiring a clear appreciation of the relative role of nationalism in explaining developments:

1. How far do you agree with the view that nationalism was of only minor importance in explaining the unification of either Italy or Germany between 1848 and 1871?

2. To what extent does the growth of Magyar nationalism explain the creation of the Dual Monarchy in 1867.
3. 'Great power politics, not nationalism, best explains the creation of nation states in the Balkans in the period 1821–1878.' How far do you agree?
4. 'Nationalism was the greatest cause of Austrian decline between 1815 and 1914.' Discuss.

Apart from question 1, all these questions require a wider perspective than the developments described in this chapter. You will need to look in chapter 3 for questions 2 and 3 and chapters 3 and 5 for question 4. What all these questions have in common, however, is the requirement that you place the role of nationalism in the context of other forces at work in shaping events. You will need to show how nationalism, whether you consider it important or not, contributed and linked in with the other forces. In question 2 you might usefully consider other nationalist movements within the Austrian Empire. In questions 2 and 4 you need to be careful to give consideration to the whole period.

5 Making Nations: The Development and Impact of Mass Nationalism, 1871–1914

POINTS TO CONSIDER

This chapter deals with a crucial period in the development of nationalism in Europe. Nationalism became a mass phenomenon, generally shifted to the right and helped bring about the First World War. You should aim to understand how nation states sought to bring about a sense of national unity, why a distinctive right wing nationalism developed and what impact nationalism had on international relations.

KEY DATES

1870–71	Franco-Prussian War.
1871	Paris Commune.
1872–78	*Kulturkampf* in Germany.
1874–1880	Disraeli Prime Minister of GB.
1890	Fall of Bismarck.
1894	Start of Dreyfus Affair.
1896	Italian defeat at Adowa.
1897	Start of *Weltpolitik*.
1908	Young Turk Revolution.
	Austria annexes Bosnia.
August 1914	Start of First World War.

In August 1914 Europe went to war. In the capitals around Europe cheering crowds welcomed the move, few resisted the call to arms and many volunteered. Politicians of every hue put differences to one side and joined in support of the national effort. Even socialists with their internationalist ideology ('workers of the world unite') rallied to the flag. What had brought about this sense of national unity and purpose? What role did nationalism play in bringing Europe to the tragedy of war? This chapter examines how states sought to foster a national consciousness and the kinds of image of the nation they sought to propagate. It also seeks to explain the rightward shift of nationalism – away from the radical and revolutionary nationalism of the first half of the nineteenth century towards a conservative, aggressive and increasingly intolerant ideology. The final objective is to indicate the ways in which nationalism affected and shaped international politics before 1914.

1 Making Nations

> **KEY ISSUES** What image of the nation did states seek to promote? How was a sense of national identity and national consciousness developed?

After the declaration of the Kingdom of Italy in 1861, the Italian nationalist and politician D'Azeglio starkly summed up the problem facing the new Italian state: 'We have made Italy, now we must make Italians'.[1] This was a major problem for the new Italian state but was not unique to Italy. For the bulk of the nineteenth century nationalism was largely a middle class phenomenon, but by the early twentieth century nationalism had penetrated the masses. This was in no small part due to the conscious action of governments. All states, new or old, in the second half of the nineteenth century were concerned to develop a sense of national identity in the mass of their people. This was partly out of a genuine belief in the 'principle of nationality' and the sense of community, pride and common endeavour it could engender. But it was, also, because loyalty to the nation, as represented by the state, could be a source of stability in a period when social and economic pressures like population growth, urbanisation and new political forces (like socialism) seemed to threaten that stability. However, if governments were actively to develop a sense of nationhood they needed to have a clear idea of the values and characteristics of the nation they were trying to promote. Here they could draw on the elements of national identity already developing within the people.

a) What Image of the Nation did Governments Seek to Promote?

Generalisations are difficult because different states wished to create their own unique identities that drew on their own unique versions of their histories, traditions and cultures. And it is important to realise that governments did not have a free hand in creating their national image. The French state could not ignore the profound effect of the humiliation suffered at the hands of Prussia in 1870–71; Italian and German nationalism was affected by the newness of the creation of the nation state and a sense of inferiority to well-established states like Britain and France. Britain's national identity, on the other hand, was rooted in an awareness of its position in the world, its naval and imperial might and the supposed supremacy of its institutions and economy.

The compound of national values and images promoted by governments has been referred to as 'state nationalism' or 'official nationalism', to distinguish it from other versions of nationalism which developed to complement or rival that of the established state. Because generalisations are difficult perhaps this state-sponsored nationalism can best be demonstrated by examination of three examples.

i) Germany

In German schools the Germans were portrayed as an *urvolk*, the bearers of a higher civilisation passed on to them by the Greeks and the Romans; they were a chosen people, the ideal bearers of civilisation with an innate superiority and pureness of blood. Germany had a mission to play a prominent role in world affairs. Under William II, promoted as a youthful and vigorous figurehead, the nation was identified with the imperial dynasty and with Prussian values of order, authoritarianism and the military. The last was very important. Indeed the historian A.J.P. Taylor referred to a 'Sadowa-Sedan' complex at the heart of German national culture, reflecting the military means by which Germany was unified.

ii) France

France appeared divided over the exact nature of its national identity. The reasons here lie not so much in the nature of its creation – France had been a relatively territorially unified state since the Middle Ages – but in the legacy of the Revolution of 1789, the vicissitudes of French politics during the nineteenth century, the humiliation delivered by defeat in the Franco-Prussian War and the trauma caused by the crushing of the Paris Commune. However, the French were presented by republican governments after 1871 as the most civilised nation, the bastion of human progress and culture, and the home of enlightened values. This was the legacy of the Revolution: France portrayed as the home of liberty and equality, a secular state that was tolerant and progressive. Governments were also keen to promote the French as a martial people, a nation of warriors who would one day exact revenge – *revanche* – on Germany for the loss of Alsace-Lorraine.

iii) Britain

Britain, of course, was neither a newly created nation state nor had it suffered recently the traumas of national defeat and civil war. What is more, it was in the 1870s the world's greatest trading nation and the possessor of the world's biggest empire; it also benefited from an established constitution. Disraeli summed up this view of nationhood in his Crystal Palace speech of 1872 when he declared that the English (in this sense a synonym for British) people were:

> ... proud of belonging to an imperial country, and are resolved to maintain, if they can, their empire – that they believe on the whole that the greatness and the empire of England [the British Empire] are to be attributed to the ancient institutions of the land.[2]

Disraeli also capitalised on the growing popularity of the monarchy by agreeing to Queen Victoria assuming the title of Empress of India in

1876, so symbolising the identity between nation and empire. Schulze described Disraeli's action as a 'masterstroke in the consolidation of the nation'.[3]

The key feature of the British worldview was the conviction that the British had a special talent for government and an imperial mission to rule and bring civilisation to the world. The British vision was that of a confident nation, proud of its freedoms, certain of the perfection of its institutions, and sure of its place in the world. It was a portrayal which perhaps was partly a reaction to the increasing challenges to its position from states like Germany and the USA.

The link between the nation and empire was to be reinforced in schools with classrooms adorned with maps of the world with the Empire in pink; in popular songs and music such as 'Rule Britannia'; in the music halls (where a popular song gave us the word jingoism to describe blind national fervour); in the arts and architecture; and the popular press. The *Daily Express* in its first issue in 1896 proclaimed that it was 'neither the mouthpiece of a political party nor the instrument of any social clique . . . Our policy is patriotic, our policy is the British Empire'.[4]

b) How did Governments Seek to Promote this National Image?

In this period governments began to take positive action to integrate their people and to create a sense of national identity and loyalty. Across Europe the strategies used by governments had some common features. These included, most importantly, the development of a system of state elementary education to communicate national identity and encourage loyalty to the state, systems of army conscription, and the introduction of national symbols, festivals, heroes and anthems.

The last quarter of the nineteenth century witnessed a massive extension of state primary education. In 1880 in Britain attendance at primary school was made compulsory and in 1888 in France. Italy provided for state elementary education in 1877 and Belgium in 1879. By 1901 Germany was spending 12 per cent of its national budget on education, England 10 per cent and France 8 (the figures were much lower for southern and eastern Europe).

Whilst the needs of the economy were a key motive behind the expansion of secondary education, the prime aim of elementary education was national integration – to turn the people into loyal citizens of the nation state. Jules Ferry, the minister responsible for developing a national system of state education in the 1880s in France, told teachers that their task was 'to prepare a generation of good citizens for our country'.[5] His colleague, Gréard, emphasised that 'in history we must emphasise only the essential features of the development of French nationality'.[6] Schools were to be engines of indoctrination – to spread the nationalist message and to develop the civic virtues of loyalty, discipline, patriotism and devotion to duty.

In Germany education policy was largely in the hands of the individual German states, but a General German School Union was formed in 1881 to promote the German language and German culture. From 1889 Prussian school history textbooks were to be written in a manner supportive of the existing order (by downplaying the role of liberals in the events of 1848, for instance, and playing up the role of the Prussian king). Increasingly throughout Germany the teaching of provincial history declined and that of a national German history prevailed.

One key aspect of education was the teaching of the national language. In Italy in the early 1860s, for instance, it is estimated that only 2.5 per cent of the people spoke Italian, and even in France in the 1870s it is estimated that only about 50 per cent of the population spoke French. For states which contained significant national minorities with a developing sense of national consciousness, however, the enforcement of a 'foreign' language was a major source of conflict. Hungary, for instance, imposed the teaching of Magyar in 1879 despite the large minorities of Serbs, Slovenes and Rumanians. Paradoxically such policies produced a backlash and contributed to the awakening of national consciousness amongst those very groups and so reduced the chances of national integration. In Russia, for example, the imposition of the Russian language in Polish areas led to the development of underground schools whose medium was the Polish language. In Austria, the teaching of Czech in Bohemia became a major concern of Czech nationalists.

If governments saw schools as a key element in educating peasants into Frenchmen or Germans or Italians, then military service was the university which consolidated that learning. Most European states, apart from Britain, had been developing systems of military service since the Napoleonic wars, but the size of armies had tended to increase over the century and the tendency towards more or less universal conscription grew. Two, three or four years' service followed by a number of years in the reserve helped to maximise a state's military capacity, but also provided a key mechanism for breaking down localism and regionalism and for inculcating national values. In Germany, the army was held in particularly high esteem because of its decisive role in establishing the German Empire. Hagen Schulze has suggested that military service was the 'most effective instrument of the national integration of Germany'.[7] But the nationalism it fostered was one intimately bound up with militarism as much as with loyalty to the state and Emperor.

Paradoxically in France, too, the army was held high in respect, despite the defeat of 1870–71. This was partly because the divisions in national politics meant that the army became the most important symbol of national unity and was the means of hope of revenge against Germany. It was certainly regarded as the 'school for the nation' in the two decades after 1871; and one minister of War, General André, emphasised its educative function: 'The regiment is more than a family. It is a school. The officer is the extension of the teacher, the nation's instructor'.[8] The lessons the army taught were those of patriotism and sacrifice. When military service became universal in France in 1889 the potency of the army as an engine for promoting national values was all the more important.

One further and important way of creating a sense of national identity was to provide national foci with which people could readily identify. Towards the end of the nineteenth century many states developed their own distinctive national symbols and imagery, alongside national festivals, the identification and celebration of national heroes (in statues, for instance) and national anthems. In France the 'Marseillaise' (see page 15) was made the national anthem in 1879. In 1880 July 14 (Bastille Day) became the national holiday and the Eiffel Tower was built to celebrate the centenary of the French Revolution in 1889. In Britain, Britannia came to symbolise Great Britain, Queen Victoria became a focus for national loyalty, and 'God Save the Queen' became the national anthem. In Germany, national imagery included the figure *Germania,* whilst the eagle, oak leaves, laurel wreaths and winged Victory became the recurrent features of the official art that adorned government buildings and railway stations.

c) What Other Factors Contributed to the Development of National Identity Amongst the Masses?

Whilst deliberate state action did much to foster a particular sense of national identity, other developments were making people conscious of the fact that they belonged to and were affected by a national community. These factors included increasing democratisation of states, increasing involvement of central government in people's lives, the development of newspapers, industrialisation, urbanisation, and the development of national road and railway networks.

First, parliamentary institutions of various kinds developed across western and central Europe in the period before the First World War. These assemblies were a bridge between the people and more or less strong centralised governments. France had universal male suffrage from 1871. In Britain the Reform Acts of 1867 and 1884 extended the vote to about 5 million adult males (about 75 per cent of the total adult male population). Germany had universal male suffrage, even if the elected Reichstag had limited powers. Austria adopted universal male suffrage in 1907, but Hungary limited the franchise to only about 5 per cent of the population, with the weight on the side of Magyar nationals. In Italy the franchise remained severely limited until 1912 – even after the reform of 1882 only about 7 per cent of the population had the vote. Whatever the differences in the size of the electorates or the powers of the institutions they elected the trend to democratisation was clear. Shrewd politicians like Disraeli in Britain, Bismarck in Germany, Gambetta in France and Giolitti in Italy recognised the need to appeal to the masses. They also recognised that the masses could be persuaded to support the state by relatively conservative and nationalist policies.

Secondly, in the last quarter of the nineteenth century more people were more directly affected by government than ever before. Governments began to take a role in regulating the workplace, providing for public health, in conscripting people for the army and in educating children. By 1914 governments were also becoming increasingly involved in providing for the poor and those in need, with schemes of national insurance, provision of pensions and unemployment benefit. For example, in Germany Bismarck introduced limited medical treatment (1883), accident and sickness insurance (1884) and pensions (1889) in an attempt to woo workers from the socialist camp and bind them to the Empire. Meanwhile, in Britain, following the second Reform Act of 1867, there was a burst of social legislation in the 1870s which built on factory, public health and education legislation earlier in the century. However, it was not until after the 1905 general election, which brought in a reforming Liberal government, that Britain followed Germany's example by introducing schemes of national insurance. Part of the stimulus here was the poor health of troops recruited for the Boer War (1899–1902). This persuaded many that a modern state needed to ensure a healthy population in the interests, as some socialists and liberals put it, of 'national efficiency'. It also reflected a shift in Liberal opinion away from laissez-faire towards intervention to better the condition of the working classes.

Thirdly, as states sought to promote a sense of national loyalty and literacy rates increased, the role of the popular press in informing and shaping public opinion became more important. A middle class press had been in existence for some time. Such a press included, for example, the *Daily Telegraph* (Britain), *Le Matin* (France), *Neueste Nachrichten* (Germany), and *Messaggiero* (Italy). However, the last decades before the First World War saw a blossoming of the so-called Yellow Press – the early twentieth century equivalent of tabloid newspapers – whose market was the literate lower middle and working classes rather than the upper classes. These included the *Daily Mail* and *Daily Express* (Britain) and *Le Petit Journal* (France). These newspapers, especially the more populist, whipped up public opinion and played to their prejudices. They thrived on vivid accounts of world politics, campaigns against scandals and tirades against foreign governments. The role of the press in the age of mass nationalism had an early demonstration in Bismarck's publication of the Ems Telegram in 1870 (see page 70).

Finally, in great measure, what made mass nationalism possible were developments associated with urbanisation and communications. Urbanisation and the drift of population from country to town eroded parochialism. Above all, the spread of railways brought countries together by facilitating the development of a 'national' economy and by breaking down local and regional barriers. Railways (and roads) were the arteries binding the various regions and localities together, facilitating the development not only of national markets but also of national communication and interaction.

2 Nationalism and Threats to Stability: National Minorities and Socialism

> **KEY ISSUE** How did states deal with the problems posed by national minorities and socialism?

For much of the nineteenth century nationalism had been seen as the ideology of the left, associated with liberalism, in a desire to overthrow conservative regimes in order to create states which reflected the wishes of the nation. The unifications of Germany and Italy and the creation of the Dual Monarchy of Austria-Hungary helped transform this position. Once 'nation states' had been produced, nationalism stopped being an ideology of reform and became one about defending the nation state. We have seen how nation states sought to propagate their own vision of the nation. In many cases the governments that did this were conservative, wishing, among other things, to preserve the state against the threats to it posed by national minorities and socialism.

a) Socialism

The brief existence of the Paris Commune in 1871 was taken as evidence of the threat of international revolution posed by socialism. Socialist doctrine, based on the teachings of Karl Marx, seemed to threaten the overthrow of the ruling classes; and socialist parties, which began to grow in this period, employed rhetoric which seemed to threaten revolution. Its internationalist claims ('workers of the world unite!') seemed to threaten the existence of nation (indeed all) states. Socialism was, then, to political leaders like Bismarck, what liberalism and nationalism had been to Metternich, and, just as Metternich overestimated the threat of liberalism and nationalism, so they overestimated the threat posed by socialism and its revolutionary potential.

Concerned about the potential appeal of socialism, conservative governments adopted a variety of strategies to counter it. Quite clearly part of the purpose of actively promoting a sense of national identity was to bind all citizens into allegiance to the national state. Part of the reason why conservative elements of society became reconciled with the nation state was the way nationalism could be used as a weapon against socialism. Bismarck sought to do this, for example, in the 1880s by identifying socialism as a *Reichsfeinde* (enemy of the Empire). He persuaded the Reichstag to pass anti-socialist legislation in 1878 which banned socialist meetings, societies and publications. Another strategy was to try to reduce the attractions of socialism to workers and bind them more closely to the national state by passing legislation which improved the lot of the workers, such as Bismarck's pioneering legislation providing for accident and sickness insurance and pensions between 1883 and 1889. Other states adopted similar approaches, reasoning that the working man would feel more bound to the state if he had a stake in its preservation.

These strategies did not stop socialist parties winning support in elections (the general trend was increasing support for socialist parties) but arguably did reduce the potential for revolution. Indeed socialist parties were less anti-national than their rhetoric suggested and many became reconciled to the nation state and to seeking gradual change through the parliamentary process. When the acid test of socialism's internationalist doctrine came in 1914 socialist parties across Europe lined up behind their respective nations in support of war.

b) National Minorities

National minorities posed a problem for nation states trying to integrate their people. For Britain there was the problem of the Irish (and the Scots and Welsh); for France the Bretons and Basques; for Germany the Poles, Danes and French; for Austria and Hungary the various Slav national groups; and for Russia a range of nationalities. The dominant nationalities in each state adopted two main strategies: they either attempted to force compliance by imposing the dominant language or culture, or they attempted to appease the minority by concessions.

In Germany German governments sought to make minorities *Reichsfeinde* and to 'Germanise' them. For example, in 1883 all Poles of Russian or Austrian origin were exiled and in 1886 a Prussian Colonisation Commission was set up to settle Germans in Polish areas. In Hungary there was generally an attempt to impose the Magyar language and restrict access to posts in administration and government to Magyars. A similar approach was adopted in the Turkification policies of the Young Turks after the revolution of 1908–9.

The effect of such policies was to alienate those national minorities and stiffen their resolve to achieve some measure of independence. For example, the Magyarisation policy of Hungary led to demands by Croats for equal status with Austria and Hungary in the Monarchy (trialism as opposed to the dualism of the existing monarchy). When these ambitions were thwarted Croat nationalists became more militant and were willing to make common cause with the Serbs.

Russia, too, with its multi-national empire, felt the need to try to integrate its people and create loyalty to the Russian state. Only about half of the subjects of the Tsar were Russian. The solution, begun as we have seen with Nicholas I (see page 36), but intensified under Alexander III, was 'Russification'. This meant the suppression of local characteristics and the spread of Russian characteristics. For example, after the defeat of the Polish rebellion of 1863, Roman Catholic property was seized and Warsaw university was closed. Russian replaced Polish as the official language and Poles were replaced by Russians in government and administration. Elsewhere the Finns were subject to increasing restrictions until in 1903 their constitution was suspended; in Armenia the property of the Armenian Church was confiscated and the Russian language imposed; in the Baltic provinces (Latvia, Lithuania and Estonia) Russians came increasingly to dominate. However, it was the Russian Jews that felt the heaviest blows. The government was happy to associate the Jews with the Polish rebellion and use them as the scapegoat for other problems. The result was a series of 'pogroms' – violent attacks – on Jews and their subjection to increasing official restrictions on movement, trading and access to education.

In the Austrian half of the Dual Monarchy a different approach was adopted. Here, there were attempts by various governments to come to terms with national minorities like the Czechs. But the results were not successful. The difficulty came not so much from the Czechs as from the Germans, whose position as the dominant nationality was thereby threatened. German nationalists did all they could to thwart concessions on language and education. For example, when the Austrian government in 1897 sought to appease the Czechs by making Czech the language of administration in Bohemia, German nationalist protests (led by Schönerer) forced their withdrawal and the resignation of the Austrian minister-president. These failures encouraged Czech nationalists to see their future in an independent state and in making common cause with other Slav nationalities which increasingly looked towards Russia. The Slavic Union of 1909 united Czech, Serb, Croat, Slovene and Austro-Ukrainian deputies in the Reichstag and led to the breakdown of the parliamentary system in 1911 and the prosecution of Slav leaders.

For British governments the main nationalist problem was that of Ireland. In the 1880s Charles Stewart Parnell had forged an effective mass nationalist movement in Ireland which was able to deliver an effective Irish Home Rule Party with sufficient MPs at Westminster to hold the balance of power between Conservatives and Liberals in 1885. Gladstone, always sympathetic to liberal nationalist movements abroad, was persuaded to try to deliver limited Home Rule to Ireland. But his proposals split his own party and met with the opposition of the Conservatives, so damning the Bill and his government to defeat. Although there was a religious element to the opposition (Protestant Britain and Ulster versus Catholic Irish), for many opponents the crucial issue was that concessions to Ireland would threaten the integrity of the Empire and hence British power and prestige. Irish MPs once again held the balance of power after the 1910 election and demanded the price of Home Rule for their support of the Liberals. The issue proved even more divisive than it had done in the1880s, with the Conservatives rallying to the support of the Protestant

Unionists of Ulster. At the time of the Home Rule Bill in 1912, the issue of Ireland was the central topic in British politics and there was even the threat of civil war. No solution had emerged before 1914. However, the onset of the First World War pushed the issue back down the political agenda.

3 Nationalism and the Extreme Right

> **KEY ISSUES** To what extent and why did a distinctive right-wing nationalism develop in this period?

a) The Nature of Right-Wing Nationalism

As we have seen, nationalism became part of the armoury of the state to be used in pursuit of policies of national integration in order to imbue their peoples with a sense of loyalty to the state. But there also developed in this period a distinctive and extreme right-wing nationalism which was aggressive, intolerant and often anti-Semitic. Some of the right-wing groups that developed can be seen as the antecedents of inter-war fascism.

It is important to draw a distinction therefore between this type of nationalism and the official or state nationalism referred to above. That is not to say the two are mutually exclusive – there were a number of common features and governments were to a greater or lesser degree influenced by the pressure from the right. The manifestations of right-wing nationalism varied in their emphasis and particular characteristics from state to state, but contained some or all of the following features:

- a belief in the primacy of the nation over the individual and that the individual's first loyalty and concern was the wellbeing of the national community;
- a belief in the distinctive character, mission or purpose of the nation and its supremacy over other nations;
- a fear of other national and racial groups which might threaten the nation's existence or strength, expressed, for instance, in anti-Semitism;
- an opposition to ideas and beliefs which proposed different loyalties and a different world order, such as socialism (with its emphasis on class) and liberalism (with its emphasis on individual rights and democracy);
- a belief in the need for authoritarian government, order and stability;
- support of a strong military establishment and an assertive foreign policy;
- a rejection of the modern world of individualism, industrialisation,

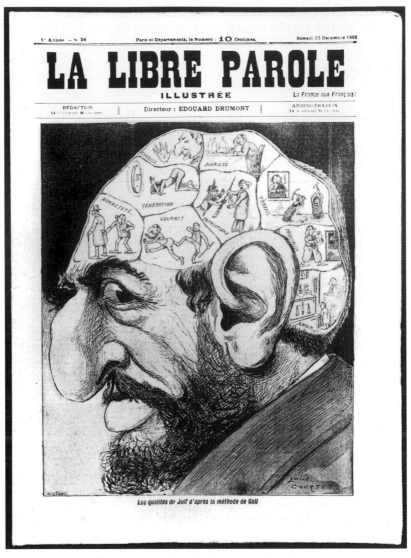

Right-wing nationalism and anti-Semitism.

A stereotypical view of the Jew, with stereotypical features:
VENERATION (love of money); HUMANITÉ (pickpocketing);
SOBRIÉTÉ (drunkenness); TRAVAIL (making others work for you);
PATRIOTISME (refusing to serve the nation).

('Jewish Virtues According to Gall's Methods' by Emile Courtet, in *La Libre Parole*,
23 December 1893.)

urban workers and large-scale capitalism in favour of an imagined ideal community based on rural life, craftsmen and peasants.

One very important influence on right-wing nationalist thinking in particular and nationalism more generally in this period was Social Darwinism. Social Darwinists, like Herbert Spencer, sought to apply the natural 'laws' described by Charles Darwin – such as survival of the fittest and the struggle for existence – to humanity. In a vulgarised form these ideas helped shape public opinion at all levels. According to Social Darwinists, competitive struggle between nations was healthy and natural; the strongest would survive; and war was not only justified but necessary. So the French thinker Georges Sorel could suggest that a foreign war would re-invigorate the French nation. General von Bernhardi's book *Germany and the next War* (1912), which was reprinted nine times by 1914, urged German politicians to view war as a moral imperative. War would cleanse the nation within and also crush the enemy without. These views were not uncommon and appeared not in obscure journals but also in the popular press and in the rhetoric of politicians.

Social Darwinism also influenced nationalism by suggesting that some races were naturally superior to others. This had three effects: outside Europe, it could justify the acquisition of colonies on the grounds that superior 'white' races could help civilise inferior races; it could justify movements such as Pan-Germanism, which aimed to unite all Germans and protect German interests abroad; and it gave some pseudo-scientific credibility to traditional anti-Semitism which revived in this period. Whilst over much of western and central Europe the Jews had become accepted and had even achieved equal rights with other citizens, in eastern Europe they retained their cultural and ethnic distinctiveness. However, the Jews, discriminated against over the centuries, became an obvious target for nationalists influenced by racial theories and contemporary literature. For example, the sinister and repulsive Jew was a recurrent figure in literature from Dickens' Fagin in *Oliver Twist* to Feval's Schwarz in *Habits Noir*. The right-wing nationalist journal *La Libre Parole*, run by Edouard Drumont, illustrates the kind of stereotypical image peddled in anti-Semitic propaganda (see page 94).

Anti-Semitism could easily be aroused in times of economic depression, partly because Jews held a disproportionately large percentage of positions in academic life, business and the professions, and partly because anti-Semitism in Russia drove many Jews westwards into countries like Austria and Germany. The Jews arriving from the east retained their strict orthodoxy and cultural distinctiveness and thereby appeared different and thus a threat to the purity of the nation.

Arguably right-wing nationalism took its most extreme form in Germany and Austria but was also present in France and Italy. Everywhere it helped shape national politics and policy.

i) Germany

In the early 19th century German romantic nationalists like Jahn and Arndt had placed emphasis on the German people as a cultural and ethnic community (a *volk*), a people with a common spirit and who were unique and innately superior. The pseudo-scientific racial theories propagated by J.A. Gobineau (*Essay on the Inequality of Races*, 1854) and H.S. Chamberlain (*The Foundations of the Nineteenth Century*, 1899) suggested further that the German race was naturally superior but needed to be protected from inferior races such as the Jews. The German writer Langbehn emphasised the superiority of German blood and saw Germany's destiny as ruler of the world. Langbehn and other German intellectuals claimed that the German landscape, especially the forests, helped shape the German people; their unique virtues were embodied in the rural way of life and in the peasantry, uncorrupted by urbanisation and the modern world. German nationality was thus rooted in 'the blood and the soil' (*blut und boden*).

These ideas blended with other right-wing ideas – the rejection of democracy, anti-socialism, suspicion of Catholicism, opposition to non-German minorities like the Poles in Posen, and antipathy to foreigners and 'foreign' ideas. To such right-wingers, the new German Empire, however successful economically, was lacking the vital element of a unifying German spirit – an overarching belief in the nation. They envisaged Germany as a *Volksgemeinschaft*, a people's community, which would put the nation first. In this ideal community all artificial divisions of class, party and religion would be eliminated. The right also viewed German unification in 1871 as incomplete; there were other Germans in Europe – not least in Austria. Moreover Germany had not yet fulfilled her destiny to become a world power. If Germany was passive she would be encircled by hostile powers. Germany must stand up for herself and protect her interests across the world.

Such ideas attracted those dissatisfied with the disunity within the new German Empire, resentful of the pressures of industrial society, and frustrated with Germany's international position. Support came especially from amongst the lower middle class – the *mittelstand* of shopkeepers and craftsmen – and from professionals like teachers and civil servants.

This right-wing nationalism found voice in a number of right-wing pressure groups which exerted a good deal of influence over the German government – the Navy League, the Colonial League, the Pan German League, the German Middle Class Association, the German Defence League and the Eastern Marches Association.

Whilst it is difficult to establish a direct link between the ultra-nationalism expressed by such groups and policy pursued by the government, some historians (like William Carr) accept that through their propaganda, wide membership and mass support, the right-wing groups 'exerted more influence on the government than did the Reichstag'.[9]

ii) France

In France right-wing nationalism developed amongst those opposed to the Third Republic, which established itself after the Franco-Prussian war and the suppression of the Paris Commune. Like its German counterpart, French right-wing nationalism was authoritarian, militarist, anti-socialist and anti-Semitic. It drew less on racial theory and appealed more to pre-Revolutionary French culture and history. It attracted a range of people disaffected by the Third Republic with its seemingly corrupt politicians, its weak pursuit of revenge against Germany and its failure to crush socialism. As in Germany, it was in some ways a reaction against the development of socialism and against the modern and modernising world with its material outlook and its liberal, individualist creed. There was an emphasis on the perceived external and internal threats to France and the French nation and, as in Germany, 'the Jew' was often blamed. The ideas of Maurice Barrés and Charles Maurras formed the core of French right-wing nationalism at the end of the nineteenth century. Barrés believed that the spirit of the French nation was not the Republican (official) nationalism taught in schools, but was rooted in the French people, in the instinct of the masses which was shaped by 'the soil and the dead' – environment and heredity. Only when France recognised this would France recover her greatness. Maurras was essentially a monarchist. He believed that the nation, as the supreme political reality, needed renewing by the purging of the forces which had debilitated it since 1789 – democracy, individualism and socialism. Frenchmen should place France above all. But this France, according to Maurras, was one derived from its monarchical and Catholic heritage, with its heroes like Clovis, Charlemagne and Joan of Arc, rather than the French Revolution.

In terms of the history of nationalism, Maurras is important because he coined the term 'integral nationalism' to describe the idea that the nation should take precedence over all other loyalties and demanded the total obedience of the individual to the state. Such integral nationalism is reflected in contemporary slogans like 'France above all' and 'My country, right or wrong!' This was an idea which fed into totalitarian thinking after the First World War.

As in Germany, these ideas found an audience amongst the lower middle classes and those working in the professions and became popular in the 1890s and 1900s. However, Maurras' *Action Française* only reached a mass audience after 1908 when a periodical of the same name was distributed on the streets by his volunteer force of 'partisans of the king' (*Camelots du roi*). As in Germany, right-wing nationalism was closely associated with the army, both because of the sympathy it enjoyed amongst the officer corps and because right-wing nationalists saw the army as the defender of national prestige. Although the Third Republic had sought to play up the importance of the army in the 1870s, the strength of its support had lessened in the 1880s as the mood of revenge waned and French foreign policy looked less to Alsace and more to colonial acquisition in North Africa and South East Asia; many in the officer corps resented this and so were attracted to militarist right-wing nationalism. In the 1890s the Dreyfus case brought the differences between the army and the government of the Third Republic to a head. In 1894 Captain Alfred Dreyfus, a Jewish officer with a German sounding name, was found guilty of treason for betraying secrets to the Germans. When, in the late 1890s, the Republican government failed to stand full square behind the army over its conviction of Dreyfus, the right wing and the army found a common cause – defence of the national interest as represented by the army. Despite evidence to the contrary, the army maintained the conviction, supported by the anti-Semitic and nationalist right-wing press. It was Emile Zola's letter, *J'accuse*, published in 1898, which stoked the fires of political controversy. He argued that Dreyfus was the victim of reactionary right-wing forces, the Catholic Church and the military. This polarised opinion in France, with the left, the Dreyfusards, taking up the cause of Dreyfus in the name of the 'Rights of Man', and the right, the 'anti-Dreyfusards', opposing the left in the name of national unity and the great national institutions, the army and the Church. The right also believed that there was a great Jewish conspiracy which sought to whitewash Dreyfus' guilt, even after the real guilty officer, Esterhazy, admitted his crime. Anti-Semitic riots and nationalist demonstrations broke out in a number of towns across France in 1898. When Dreyfus was re-tried in 1899 the issue appeared less Dreyfus' guilt or innocence than the army's and, by association, the nation's 'honour'. In the event Dreyfus was pardoned by the government, but the furore stimulated by the case had split French politics down the middle, and the ensuing battle waged between left and the right has been described as a 'battle for the soul of the nation'.[10]

iii) Austria-Hungary

It was in Austria-Hungary, particularly in Austria, that some of the most virulent right-wing nationalism developed. In the Austrian part of the Dual Monarchy Germans comprised about 36 per cent of the population; the proportion was broadly similar in the Czech provinces of Austria. In statistical terms, therefore, the Germans were another national minority in Austria. Whilst historically they had been effectively the dominant national group, now that position was not so secure. The demands of Czechs both for equal language rights in government and for Czech schools threatened the traditional monopoly of German; the Czechs were also improving their social and economic position in Bohemia in industry and commerce. What is more, the defeat of 1866 had for the first time effectively cut Austrian Germans from those in the new German Empire. Perhaps the Austrian monarchy was no longer the reliable guarantor of German superiority. To this sense of vulnerability was added the potent influence of Social Darwinism and race theories.

In the 1880s an extreme German nationalism developed which played on anti-Semitism and looked to fellow Germans in the German Empire. This Pan-German movement in Austria was lead by Georg von Schönerer. He campaigned for the retention of German as the sole official language of the Austrian monarchy, viewed Slavs and Jews as enemies within the state and hinted at the union of German areas with the German Empire. He famously campaigned for the national-isation of a Jewish-owned railway. This Pan-German movement attracted vociferous support mainly from students and Germans in areas where Slavs and Jews were numerous – i.e. where Germans felt particularly vulnerable.

One other Austrian German who successfully played the anti-Semitic card was Carl Lueger, who was elected mayor of Vienna in 1895. There was a large Jewish minority in Vienna and, as in other places, they were disproportionately represented in academic, pro-fessional and business life. Vienna had also suffered an influx of Russian Jews, escaping the pogroms. Lueger argued for the exclusion of Jews from public, professional and business life and won consider-able support amongst the middle class. In the 1897 general election his Christian Social Party played heavily on popular prejudice and swept the board in Vienna. Lueger is also significant because of his effect on the young Adolf Hitler, a down and out in Vienna in the years preceding the First World War.

iv) Italy

In Italy right-wing nationalism did not develop in the same way or to the same extent as in Germany or France. Issues of race were far less prominent, although there was an assumption of Italian cultural supe-riority. Right-wing nationalism had its roots in a sense of frustration with Italian liberalism and hence a desire for authoritarian govern-ment. Italian nationalists longed to incorporate areas of Italian nationality as yet outside the Italian kingdom (*Italia irredenta*), like the Trentino and Trieste, hoped to win colonies, and feared socialism. Writers like Turiello in the 1880s argued that Italian national con-sciousness needed to be aroused by military enterprise through the conquest of colonies. Politicians like Rocco de Zerbi maintained that Italy needed rejuvenating through war – 'a bath of blood'.[11] A key focus was the acquisition of colonies in Africa, especially after France annexed 'Italian' Tunis in 1882. Crispi was the first Prime Minister to seek to appease right-wing opinion by launching an attack on Abyssinia, an attempt that led to disastrous defeat at Adowa in 1896.

Nationalist hopes were raised and then dashed by this humiliating failure and the sense of national weakness stimulated the growth of a distinctive right-wing nationalism after 1900. There was a spate of right-wing journals – *L'idea Nazionale, Mare Nostrum, La Grande Italia* – and by 1910 a Nationalist Party had emerged. It had some things in common with right-wing parties elsewhere in Europe – it was anti-democratic, anti-socialist, bellicose and imperialist and, to some degree, anti-Semitic. It was also influenced by Social Darwinist ideas about struggle between nations. An Italian right-wing nationalist, Alfredo Rocco, summed up the Italian version of right-wing nationalism in the following way:

> Nationalism attacks democracy, demolishes anti-clericalism, fights socialism and undermines pacifism, humanitarianism and internationalism. It declares the programme of liberalism finished.[12]

Right-wing nationalists welcomed the Italian government's decision to conquer Libya in 1911–12 and viewed victory as a testament to Italy's national prowess. It was such views which made the policy of neutrality when war broke out in 1914 untenable in the long run; the only decision to make was which side to join. Here, too, the prospect of gaining *Italia irredenta*, Balkan territory and colonies threw the nationalist voice behind alliance with Britain and France.

4 Nationalism and International Relations

> **KEY ISSUE** What impact did nationalism have on international politics?

What follows seeks to indicate the various ways in which nationalism influenced international relations. It focuses on the renewed drive to colonial empire (often referred to as the 'new imperialism'), the increasing rivalry and tension between states, and the impact of Balkan nationalism in the build-up to the First World War.

a) The New Imperialism

Between the 1870s and the outbreak of the First World War, many European states became involved in a competition to gain colonies. The French carved an Empire in North and West Africa as well as in South-East Asia; the Germans gained colonies in Africa and in the Pacific; the British extended their already vast Empire across much of Africa; the Italians sought imperial power in the horn of Africa and Libya; the Russians pushed their empire into central and eastern Asia; and even the Belgians grabbed the Congo. The reasons for the renewed burst of colonial acquisition from the 1870s can be partly explained by the growth of nationalism in Europe. Indeed imperialism has sometimes been described as the turning outwards of the national state mentality.

In general terms, possession of colonies was seen as a way of increasing a nation's prestige. For the Republican governments of France in the 1880s colonial acquisition seemed a way of restoring national pride without war with Germany over Alsace-Lorraine. Indeed there is some evidence that Germany encouraged this policy (especially the acquisition of Tunis in 1882). For Italy colonial acquisition was seen as a means of showing itself to be a great power. In Germany's case, many saw the acquisition of colonies as proof of its national prestige and of its claim to rival Great Britain.

By the 1890s the scramble for colonies had become first and foremost a struggle for power and a test of national vigour. Clashes over territory could have an important impact on domestic politics. When the British forced a French climb-down in the Sudan at Fashoda in 1898, right-wing nationalists in France did not blame the army but the enemy within which discredited the army and divided and weakened France. (This was at the height of the Dreyfus Affair.)

b) National Rivalry

Nationalism put a premium on notions of national honour, prestige and glory. Crises in international relations tended to become issues of national prestige and national greatness. For one reason or another, apart from Britain and perhaps Russia, the nation states of Europe were motivated generally by a sense of inferiority or humiliation, or a desire to prove themselves. What is more, foreign policy could be seen as a way of diverting attention from domestic problems and of uniting the people behind the national interest. This was, of course, a potentially high-risk strategy. Whilst success offered the potential for domestic peace, humiliation or defeat could further destabilise society at home.

The connection between domestic affairs and foreign policy was intimate and is perhaps best illustrated by the German pursuit of *weltpolitik* under William II. *Weltpolitik*, or world policy, aimed to make German a world power. In explaining this policy in 1897 Chancellor von Bulow said: 'I am putting the main emphasis on foreign policy. Only a successful foreign policy can help to reconcile, pacify, rally, unite'.[13] *Weltpolitik*'s domestic purpose was to unite national opinion and neutralise the growing influence of socialism. A second strand of this policy was a protectionist economic policy, to protect German farmers, coupled with a naval building programme which helped heavy industry. It was also hoped that the latter aspect would also help bring the workers round in support of the state rather than being attracted to socialism.

The naval building programme can also be seen as a strand of *weltpolitik* in that a strong navy was seen as essential to Germany's international prestige and the pursuit of colonies. Germany looked jealously on the empires of Britain and France, sought colonies itself and demanded the right to be consulted in colonial affairs. Germany, like other European powers, won a treaty port in China (Kiaochow) and purchased some Pacific islands from Spain in 1899. More important was the building of the Berlin to Baghdad railway which secured German influence in the Ottoman Empire, a project which aroused the concern of both Russia and Britain. Britain was also concerned at what was seen as Germany's unwarranted intervention in South Africa when the Kaiser, in the Kruger telegram, appeared to offer support to the Boers after the Jameson Raid (1896). Germany's naval building programme, begun under Admiral Tirpitz in 1898, was an even more serious concern. Meanwhile France was angered by Germany's attempts to muscle in on French interests in Morocco (1905 and 1911). Whilst these German actions have the distinct mark of the Kaiser himself, they were also encouraged by nationalists in the Naval League, the Pan-German League and the Colonial League.

Popular aggressive nationalism was also a feature of Britain and France in the years before 1914. In France, the Moroccan crisis of 1911 was resolved in part by French concession of part of their Congo possessions to Germany. This 'humiliation', as the right portrayed it, aroused popular anger which fed on other sources of hostility to Germany (such as the latent desire for revenge over Alsace-Lorraine) and added to the climate of friction preceding 1914. In Britain the temper of public opinion can be gauged by the crowds chanting 'We want war!' outside Buckingham Palace on 3 August 1914.

That is not to say popular nationalism drove governments into war in 1914, but the presence of a significant and vociferous element of public opinion supporting an aggressive stance removed one potential obstacle in the way of a decision for war.

c) Balkan Nationalism and the Origins of the First World War

At the start of the twentieth century, as had been the case for much of the nineteenth century, instability in the Balkans threatened to destabilise Europe. In 1903 the Serbian monarch, who had been subservient to Austrian interests, was assassinated by Serb nationalists who wanted to create a greater Serbia to include all Serbs. The new nationalist regime looked not to Vienna but to St Petersburg for support. In this way, to Austrian eyes, Serbia threatened to become the Balkan 'Piedmont' with Russia potentially playing the role of France. Just as France fought Austria in 1859 to help Piedmont, Russia might fight Austria in order to increase the power of Serbia. This, and the growing assertiveness of Croats and Serbs in the Dual Monarchy, helped prompt Austria to take advantage of the Young Turk revolt in 1908 and of Russian weakness following her defeat against Japan in 1905 to annex Bosnia-Herzogovina. This, on the one hand, was an assertion of Austrian power and, on the other, a clear attempt to stifle Serbian ambitions. Austria was also to take advantage of Albanian nationalism to restrict Serbian expansion. In 1910 and 1911 Albania revolted against the Young Turk government's Turkification policies and in 1912 declared its independence from the Ottoman Empire. Austria seized this opportunity of reducing the possibility of Serbia achieving access to the Adriatic by recognising Albania's independence and by threatening force if Serbia continued its siege of the Albanian city of Scutari. Austria was now committed to a course of no compromise with Serb (and other Slav) nationalist ambitions which threatened her Empire.

The collapse of the authority of the Ottoman Empire affected not only Albania. Other Balkan states saw an opportunity for territorial expansion. In 1912 Serbia, Montenegro, Greece and Bulgaria formed the Balkan League and attempted to throw the Turks out of mainland Europe. This was successful but the winners fell out over the spoils and, in a second Balkan War in 1913, Serbia, Greece and Rumania attacked and defeated Bulgaria. The result was a 'big Serbia', stronger and, worryingly for Austria, apparently determined to realise her nationalist ambitions.

Austrian acquisition of Bosnia had angered Russia which, defeated in Asia, was concerned not to be further humiliated in the Balkans. Serbia looked to Russia for protection and Russia was prepared to offer it. Meanwhile Serbian success in 1913 had made Austria more keen to deal with the Serbian problem when – and if – an opportunity arose.

5 Conclusion: Nationalism in 1914

> **KEY ISSUE** How far was there national unity when war was declared in 1914?

The traditional picture of European opinion in August 1914 suggests that the outbreak of war was popular and that governments had little difficulty in arousing national enthusiasm. Film footage of crowds in capital cities demonstrating their support for war, the hundreds of thousands of volunteers for Kitchener's Army in Britain, the German student regiments which met their deaths in the battle for Ypres in November 1914, all seem to testify to the strength of national loyalty and patriotism amongst the peoples of Europe. This view is reinforced by the willingness even of socialist parties to support their nation rather than the cause of the international working class: the German socialists voted for war credits in August 1914; the French socialists joined in the Sacred Union declared by President Poincaré to defend France; and the Labour Party in Britain gave the government no trouble and would later join a coalition government. Mobilisation, too, went ahead everywhere with little difficulty – very few resisted the call to arms.

This picture of nations united behind their governments needs some qualification, however. Little detailed study has been done on public opinion in 1914, but a French historian has suggested that the response to mobilisation and war in a number of areas was not enthusiasm, but tears and consternation.[14] In London, the socialist Beatrice Webb noted a 'strained solemnity on every face' on 5 August.[15] Certainly the young men who volunteered in their droves in Britain in 1914 appear to have done so for a mixture of motives, not solely for reasons of patriotism. War offered adventure and an escape from the factory and the mine. It was also assumed, of course, that the war would be short, relatively bloodless and victorious.

Whether the general situation was one of enthusiasm or mere acceptance, the present state of evidence suggests that by 1914 nationalism had so permeated the peoples of Europe that they did rally to the national cause. In that sense national war did provide a diversion from other divisive domestic issues such as Home Rule for Ireland in Britain and socialism in Germany. In the face of a foreign threat the nation took priority over other loyalties. James Joll concluded that 'it is certain that for a brief period in August 1914 ... war made people forget their differences and created a sense of national unity in each country, so that in French villages the *curé* [priest] and the schoolteacher spoke to each other for the first time, and, in the Reichstag in Berlin, socialist deputies attended the Kaiser's reception'.[16] Whilst the internal divisions and frictions still existed, then, they were not sufficient to prevent a united front in the face of a foreign threat.

But how far do these points suggest that nationalism was deeply embedded in the people? Was it only under the threat and reality of war that national enthusiasm could be aroused? And did the national flag and the prospect of war merely provide both a cloak to hide the more significant long term divisions within society, and an opportunity to escape from the relentless problems and frustrations of life in the industrial age?

Arguably, however, the lack of significant opposition to war in 1914 is a testimony to the success of policies of national integration pursued in the previous decades, to the sense of national community that had developed, and to the effect of right-wing nationalism in promoting an aggressive, xenophobic and intolerant nationalism which tended to view war as natural and desirable. The First World War was to be above all a war of nations, a war of each nation against its national enemy. For Austria it was a war against Serbia, for Germany a war against Russia, for France and Britain a war against Germany. It was a war in which the national loyalty of the people was called upon, exploited and tested to the extreme.

References

1 Quoted in E.J. Hobsbawm, *Age of Capital, 1848–1875* (Abacus,), p. 111.
2 R. Gildea, *Barricades and Borders, Europe, 1800–1914* (Oxford, 1996), p. 223.

3 H. Schulze, *States, Nations and Nationalism* (Blackwell, 1996), p. 241.
4 Ibid, p. 244.
5 Quoted in D.Thomson, *Europe Since Napoleon* (Penguin, 1966), p. 367.
6 Ibid, p. 367.
7 Schulze, *States, Nations and Nationalism*, p. 246.
8 A. Cassels, *Ideology & International Relations in the Modern World* (Routledge, 1996), p. 99.
9 W. Carr, *A History of Germany 1815–1990* (Arnold, 1991), p. 174.
10 Schulze, *States, Nations and Nationalism*, p. 236.
11 D. Mack Smith, *Modern Italy, A Political History* (Yale, 1997), p. 134.
12 Hobsbawm, *Age of Empire 1875–1914*, p. 142.
13 T.A. Morris, *European History 1848–1945* (Collins, 1995), p. 174.
14 J.J. Becker, *The Great War and the French People* (Leamington Spa, 1985) referred to in J. Joll, *The Origins of the First World War* (Longman, 1992), p. 211.
15 Quoted in J. Joll, *The Origins of the First World War* (Longman, 1992), p. 213.
16 Joll, *The Origins of the First World War*, p. 214.

Summary Diagram

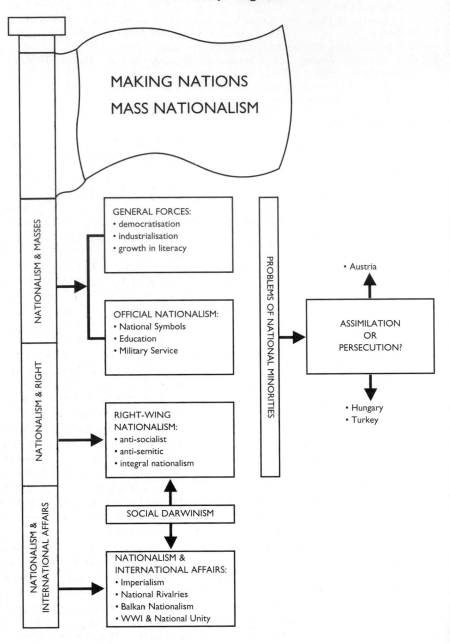

Essay questions on Chapter 5

Essay questions on nationalism in this period are likely to focus on three themes – the growth of mass nationalism, the development of right-wing nationalism and the impact of nationalism on international affairs. Consider the following essay titles:

1. To what extent was mass nationalism the creation of state governments?
2. Why did right-wing nationalist movements develop in this period?
3. How far did nationalism affect international relations in this period?

1. 'To what extent' questions require you to balance the factor identified in the question (in this case the role of state governments) against other factors that might be involved. You will need to demonstrate not only the ways that state governments sought to encourage a feeling of national loyalty and identity, but also to set this in the context of other factors more or less independent of state governments which also encouraged national feeling – such as the growth of literacy, popular journalism, increased communication, the growth of 'national' economies and societies. The question also requires you to come to a judgement about 'to what extent?' Was the role of state governments the crucial factor, or merely a contributor? Did the situation vary from state to state?

2. This Why? question clearly requires you to identify the range of important factors involved in explaining the rise of right-wing nationalism (such as fear of socialism, Social Darwinism, xenophobia, anti-Semitism, the presence of national minorities etc.). However, if that is all that you did you would not necessarily score very highly at A-level. You will also need to decide which factors were more important and which less and to show how the various factors you identify relate to each other. How important is Social Darwinism, for instance, in encouraging ideas of race, national competition and the need to outdo other nations? Again, are some factors more important in some contexts than others. Why was anti-Semitism such an element of right-wing nationalism in Austria but less so in Italy?

3. As with question 1 the requirement is that the factor identified in the question (nationalism) needs to be balanced against other factors. You will need to identify the ways in which nationalism can be said to have influenced international relations – in areas such as imperialism and the problems raised by Balkan nationalism, for instance. But you will also need to balance this analysis against other relevant factors, such as economic stimuli or traditional great power politics. Was nationalism important in all aspects of international relations, or just some? Did it have a direct bearing on particular policies or did it rather shape the context in which international relations took place?

6 Dreams and Nightmares: Nationalism 1914–45

POINTS TO CONSIDER

Nationalism had been a major cause of the First World War; it was also a major cause of the Second. This chapter examines the development of nationalism in the inter-war period. Your aim should be to understand why the application of the principle of national self-determination in the peace treaties caused so many problems and why right-wing nationalism, and especially fascism, became so dominant.

KEY DATES

1919–1920	Paris Peace Settlement.
1922	Mussolini takes power in Italy.
1929	Wall Street Crash, start of Great Depression.
1933	Hitler takes power in Germany.
1935	Italian invasion of Abyssinia; German rearmament.
1938	German union with Austria; German annexation of Sudetenland from Czechoslovakia.
1938	Germany invaded Poland; start of World War Two.
1941	German invasion of Soviet Union; start of Great Patriotic War.
1945	End of War.

1 The Experience of the Great War, 1914–18

> **KEY ISSUE** How did states use nationalism to maintain the war effort and weaken their enemies?

We have seen how states were able to exploit, and were affected by, mass nationalism in deciding on war in 1914. In general there was little opposition to the outbreak of war in 1914 and even socialist parties supported the war effort. Once war had broken out states needed to maintain popular support and needed to organise their states for war. This was more apparent once it became clear the war would not be 'over by Christmas'. In order to achieve the immense coordination of resources required for this modern, destructive and industrialised war, states needed to maintain the support of the people who would serve in its armies, make arms in its factories, drive its trains, and suffer its destruction and deprivations. The war required, therefore, an immense propaganda effort to persuade and keep persuaded the people that this was a national war where the nation's future was at

A 1914 recruitment poster. The central figure is Lord Kitchener, the Secretary of State for War and the figurehead of the recruitment campaign.

A 1915 recruitment poster. Scarborough had been bombarded by the Germans.

stake. Consider the posters on page 109, which indicate something of the call to the nation. One appeals directly to feelings of national loyalty; the other plays on xenophobic attitudes by portraying the enemy as evil.

The need for national unity meant putting internal divisions to one side. So in France, left and right united (the *union sacrée*) against the common enemy; in Britain Home Rule for Ireland and the struggle for women's suffrage were put on the back burner; in Germany, the Kaiser famously said he recognised only Germans, not parties. In the national cause, politicians were willing to grant governments wide-ranging powers to prosecute the war. In Germany, the Reichstag enthusiastically granted emergency powers to the state, and in Britain parliament passed the Defence of the Realm Act. This was the *levée en masse* of 1793 (see page 16) writ large. Governments were able in an unprecedented way to take control of the supply of raw materials, of transport, of manpower, of industrial production and of food supply (via rationing, for instance). The national effort went so far as to require the renaming of streets, towns and even families. For example, in Russia, St Petersburg became Petrograd and in Britain the royal family dropped the German Saxe-Coburg in favour of the name Windsor. In a sense, then, the war effort can be seen as the triumph of 'integral nationalism' (see page 97) as war required the total subordination of the individual to the needs of the nation as expressed by the state. The appeal was to patriotism and the defence of the nation, not, except by association (as in the case of Britain and the USA), to the defence of liberty or democracy.

In these ways nations were galvanised and accepted the war. Only towards the end of the war, under the immense strains placed on populations by the level of casualties, the massive disruption of normal life and the ravages caused by economic blockade, did the national consensus begin to crack and significant dissident anti-war voices begin to be raised.

Whilst nationalism was a potent tool for maximising the war effort at home, it was also used by both sides as a weapon to weaken their enemies. So Britain and France, for instance, sought to exploit and encourage Arab nationalism against the Turkish Empire and to encourage Serb, Croat, Slovene and Czech nationalism against Austria-Hungary. They also offered German and Austrian Poles the prospect of a nation state. For its part, Germany encouraged Polish, Finnish and Ukrainian nationalism within the Russian Empire and Irish nationalism against the British.

To some degree the strategy worked. In 1917–18 Austria-Hungary began to collapse from the inside, while in Russia the Baltic provinces (Latvia, Lithuania and Estonia) and the Finns set up national governments. The Irish nationalists, too, sought to take advantage of the war in the Easter Rising of 1916. The peacemakers who gathered at Paris in 1919, therefore, did not only have to make peace with the Central Powers, they had to try to re-draw the map of Europe to meet the demands of aspiring national groups. Their task was nothing less than the creation of a new order in central and eastern Europe.

2 Nationalism and Peace

KEY ISSUE How far did nationalism influence the making of peace in Europe?

So one of the key issues facing the peacemakers in 1919 was how to resolve the problems raised in central and eastern Europe by the desire for subject peoples to establish their own nation states following the collapse of Austria-Hungary. Promises made by the Allies during the war and the Fourteen Points of the American President Woodrow Wilson issued in January 1918 ensured that considerations of national self-determination would be prominent in the peacemaking process.

Wilson's belief in national self-determination was similar in some ways to that of the liberal nationalists of the first half of the nineteenth century, with the romantic idealism and optimism associated with it. The logic ran something like this: if each nationality was given its own state and each adopted a democratic constitution which sought to reconcile any national minorities to the new state, then an era of peace, prosperity and cooperation between states could – indeed would – ensue, with disputes being resolved peacefully through an international organisation – the League of Nations. The success of such a scheme would depend on the commitment of the members, the general acceptance of national frontiers laid down in the peace treaties and the successful assimilation of national minorities in new nation states.

Such optimism seemed hopelessly unrealistic in relation to central and eastern Europe. As we have seen, national communities did not live in neat geographically concentrated areas and any attempt to draw frontiers around the complexity of ethnic groups was bound to create large minority populations within any new nation state. What is more the creation of new states would need to take account of the history of rivalry and bitterness between different national groupings – between Germans and Czechs, Magyars and Croats, Poles and Ukrainians. Other considerations also preoccupied the peacemakers: the fear of communist revolution, the economic viability of successor states and the need for political stability.

However, the attempt was made to reorganise Europe on national lines. The peacemakers provided for an independent Poland for the Poles, Czechoslovakia for the Czechs and Slovaks, Yugoslavia for the

Europe: the territorial settlement, 1919–20.

Croats, Slovenes, and Serbs, alongside an enlarged Romania and an independent Austria and Hungary (see the map on page 112). On the positive side, the treaties reduced by almost half the number of nationals living under alien rule. What the peace treaties in effect did was to replace multi-national Austria-Hungary by a series of multi-national minor states, each with their dominant nationality, but each with more or less aggrieved national minorities. It was this negative side that was to cause the problems – around 30 million people remained living as national minorities after 1919. Poland, for example, contained some 4 million Ukrainians, 3 million Jews and over a million Germans. What is more these national minorities could all too often look to a neighbour of their own nationality. For example, the Serb problem in Bosnia for Austria-Hungary prior to 1914 was paralleled in the newly created Czechoslovakia by the Germans in the Sudetenland, the Poles in Teschen and the Hungarians in the south-east. Czechoslovakia faced the additional problem of being surrounded by relatively powerful states in Germany, Poland and Hungary.

Whilst the principle of national self-determination clearly influ enced the making of peace in central and eastern Europe, it was specifically denied to Germans. The logic of the principle would have allowed the creation of a German national state which would have united Austria and Germany. But under the terms of the Treaty of Versailles the union (*Anschluss*) between the two German states was forbidden. Clearly the peacemakers were not going to allow the creation of a potentially more powerful Germany in the centre of Europe after the ravages of four years of war. In addition, in order to give the new Polish state access to the sea, self-determination was also denied to the Germans in West Prussia and Posen, which together became the 'Polish Corridor' and a source of particular bit- terness to German nationalists. On top of all this, Germany had to take the blame for the war, pay enormous reparations, lose its over- seas empire, return Alsace-Lorraine to France and have its armed forces reduced to a nominal strength. Furthermore, the price of peace had also been the removal of the German Emperor. The sense of bitterness and humiliation this created is well-documented and associated the new democratic government in Germany (the Weimar Republic) with defeat and betrayal. Right-wing nationalists within Germany were able to win support by exploiting this sense of humili- ation.

Germany was not the only disaffected state at the end of the war. Winners and losers alike had reasons for criticism of the peace settle- ment and the economic and social dislocation caused by the war helped make politics everywhere unstable. Even before the end of the war Russia had experienced two revolutions and then – in 1918 – had descended into civil war as the communists under Lenin sought to retain their control. Poland sought to extend its territory and succeeded by force of arms in grabbing Vilna from the new state of Lithuania and also territory from Russia. Italy felt cheated out of territorial gains by the peace treaties and nationalists in protest occupied the Adriatic port of Fiume. The Turks successfully challenged the peace settlement and were able to secure the whole of present-day Turkey at the expense of the Greeks in a revised treaty (Lausanne, 1923). In France the punishment meted out to Germany was insufficient to assuage fears of renewed attack from the east. Across the new states of Europe, economic and social crisis and fear of communism threatened the survival of the newly instituted democratic forms of government. Everywhere right-wing nationalism offered an alternative of strong, authoritarian government in place of 'weak' democracy.

3 Nationalism and the New States

KEY ISSUE How far did the new states have a sense of national unity?

In 1927 the Czech leader Masaryk declared: 'the Peace treaties have created juster conditions throughout Europe, and we are entitled to expect that the tension between states and races will decrease ... The new order ... has shorn nationalism of its negative character by setting oppressed peoples on their own feet'.[1] This was certainly the hope of the peacemakers, but did it reflect the reality in the new states? Each of the new states initially had a democratic constitution that contained specific terms designed to protect the national minorities within them. Universal suffrage guaranteed them a voice. They were guaranteed citizenship, equality before the law, the right to practise their religion, their own schools and so on. A final safeguard was the right to petition the League of Nations if minorities felt persecuted. The hope was that over time the minority nationalities would become assimilated in the new state. After all, the Swiss state comprised principally both French and German speakers, the Bretons in France were reconciled to the French state, and the Scots and Welsh to the British.

On the other hand, of course, the Irish were not reconciled to the British state and were involved in a struggle with Britain to achieve independence, to a large degree granted in 1921. And, of course, the Poles in Germany, the Austrian Empire and the Russian Empire had never become assimilated. The degree of dissatisfaction felt by minorities can be illustrated by reference to the 525 petitions submitted to the League of Nations by minorities by 1931. The League machinery for dealing with these petitions was slow and in reality offered little protection. For example, in 1930-31 only 18 out of 204 petitions received were investigated. So in the main the new nation states were able to pursue policies which attempted to marginalise minority national groups with little fear of League of Nations' intervention. So, for instance, the Poles were able to close Ukrainian schools and the Rumanians Bulgarian schools. Indeed, in 1934 Poland felt strong enough to defy the League by renouncing its obligations to minorities. Everywhere across eastern Europe the Jews were discriminated against. For example, in 1920 Hungary passed a law defining the Jews as a separate race and in 1924 a Rumanian citizenship law made 100,000 Jews stateless.

Czech discrimination against Germans was by no means the worst case, but it will serve as an example of the factors at work. There was a legacy of bitterness between the Czechs and the Germans as Germans had dominated government and society in the nineteenth century. But now the position was reversed. Inevitably, perhaps, there was mutual resentment. Germans felt humiliated by the pressure to register as Czechs for the 1921 census, felt they were laid off first in times of economic hardship, suffered disproportionately from enforced land redistribution, often had to attend Czech schools and had their newspapers censored in the mid 1930s. The friction increased, of course, after Germany began a propaganda campaign in support of the Nazi Sudeten German Party and encouraged its leader, Henlein, to demand self-government.

4 Nationalism and the Soviet Union

> **KEY ISSUES** What was Soviet policy towards its national minorities? How 'Nationalist' was Soviet Communism?

The one multi-national empire to survive the First World War (albeit in a radically different form) was Russia. Under Communist rule the Soviet Union (as Russia was called by the 1920s) was able to control its various nationalities until its collapse after 1989. Then the Union disintegrated into various new nation states, and even the remaining Russian Federation is threatened by the destructive forces of Chechen and other nationalisms. It is remarkable, therefore, that a country defeated in war, subjected to a humiliating peace settlement with Germany and ravaged by first revolution and then civil war should have emerge as a relatively stable union of various nationalities in the interwar period. Why was this?

In 1917–18 the Baltic provinces of Latvia, Lithuania, Estonia and Finland had taken advantage of Russian defeat and internal chaos to set up their own governments, and other nationalities such as the Poles and Ukrainians sought independence. In the face of Allied support there was little the new communist state could do about the Baltic states and Finland, and the attempt to push the Poles back failed in the war of 1920–21. However, Lenin managed to retain control over the rest of the old Russian Empire with its various nationalities. Whilst, according to Marxist dogma, the idea of the nation and the nation state was an expression of capitalism, Lenin took a more pragmatic approach. He accepted that nationalism and national identity could not simply be legislated away. Instead the constitution of the Soviet Union (the Union of Soviet Socialist Republics) was a federal system which accepted the existence of various non-Russian nationalities. Indeed the Soviet Union allowed the use of native languages in schools and administration and produced a system which Mark Mazower has judged 'subtle, pioneering and remarkably durable'.[2] The Soviet Union opened Ukrainian schools whilst Poland was closing them.

But this is only part of the story. Whilst it is true that the Soviet Union was a federation, and that other nationalities were given rights (Stalin, a Georgian, was, under Lenin, Commissar for Nationalities), it is also true that, unlike the Germans in Austria-Hungary or the Turks in the Ottoman Empire, Russians were in the majority. It is also true that nationalism had not permeated the masses in the way that had been happening further to the west. But most importantly the Soviet Union, despite its federal structure, was a highly centralised state controlled from Moscow.

Lenin had hoped that the Bolshevik revolution in Russia would be followed by communist revolutions across Europe. But in the event the Soviet Union found itself alone in a hostile world. This led to the effective 'nationalisation' of communism, symbolised by the policy of 'socialism in one country' adopted by Stalin. To be a Russian patriot was now to be a good communist and vice versa. The requirements of the Five Year Plans and the collectivisation of agriculture were justified not only in terms of communist ideology but also in terms of national security. When war broke out with Germany in 1941, it was fought not as a crusade to save communism, but as the 'Great Patriotic War', the defence of 'Mother Russia'. One can, of course, stretch this too far. When the Germans invaded the Ukraine many people welcomed them as liberators and Stalin was worried enough by the threat posed by different national groups to order wholesale deportations to Siberia both during and after the war. The Germans of the Volga region were an obvious target, but Martin McCauley estimates that, between 1941 and 1948, about 52 nationalities were deported – over 3 million people.[3]

5 Right-Wing Nationalism and Fascism

> **KEY ISSUE** What part did nationalism play in right-wing politics and in fascism?

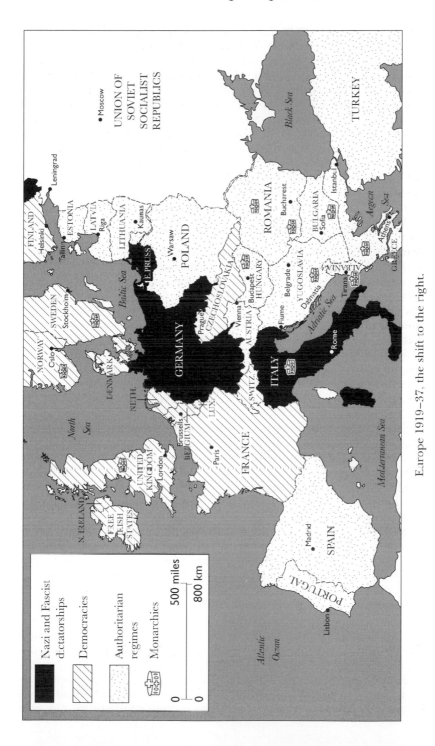

Europe 1919–37, the shift to the right.

Nazi and Fascist
dictatorships

Democracies

Authoritarian
regimes

Monarchies

In the immediate aftermath of the First World War, democracy had high prestige as the modern form of government. Every country in Europe outside the Soviet Union either already had a democratic system or was adopting one. However, within a few years the tide turned decisively against democracy. In the 1920s, Bulgaria, Hungary, Italy, Turkey, Albania, Spain, Portugal, Poland, Lithuania and Yugoslavia, and in the 1930s, Germany, Austria, Greece, Latvia, Estonia and Romania, all became right-wing dictatorships of one sort or another. Only established democracies like Britain, France, Belgium, the Netherlands, the Scandinavian countries and the new state of Czechoslovakia resisted the attractions of authoritarian government (see map on page 117).

a) The Appeal of Right-Wing Nationalism

What these new authoritarian governments had in common was their claim to be acting for the good of the nation. Some of these regimes looked backwards to a pre-democratic, pre-materialist age and sought to restore traditional conservative élites – the Church, the military, the landowners – to power. To some degree this was the politics of the Spanish nationalist leader General Franco, the Austrian leader Dollfuss, Salazar in Portugal and Metaxas in Greece. All saw the established church as the bulwark of the regime. Others sought to revolutionise society through a new right-wing vision of the nation which elevated the nation to mystical levels and which demanded the total loyalty and commitment of the people. This was a key characteristic of Fascism in Italy and Nazism in Germany. Whether one, some or all of these right-wing regimes can be classified as fascist is a matter of historical debate and largely depends on the criteria used to define fascism in the first place. What is of interest here is that the nation and the supposed interests of the nation were propounded as the legitimisation for an authoritarian regime which alone could unify the people, heal its internal divisions and defend its interests abroad.

There were a number of factors which led to the rejection of democracy. These included: the economic and social dislocation and crisis created by first the First World War; dissatisfaction with the Versailles peace settlement; the threat of communist revolution; the apparent inability of the new-fangled 'bourgeois' democracy to deal with the problems facing states; and the militarist psychology which was another legacy of war.

The war had disrupted the economy of the whole of Europe and left all the combatants heavily in debt and sometimes with a significant proportion of their productive capacity destroyed. All faced the problems of reconstruction and of adapting once more to peace-time trade. All suffered in the immediate aftermath of the war from inflation, unemployment and other related economic and social problems. Many had lost overseas markets to foreign competitors. The new states of central and eastern Europe, once part of an economy suited to a vast empire, now had to survive on their own. In addition to the economic problems came the problems associated with returning soldiers, casualties and refugees.

On top of this were the internal divisions created by, on the one hand, the apparent onward march of communism and the class-based politics of the left, and, on the other, the frictions between new national majorities and minorities. The success of the Bolshevik Revolution in Russia struck fear in the hearts of middle and upper class Europeans faced with apparently growing communist parties and working-class militancy in their own states. The first few years after 1918 saw numerous communist risings on a national or local level in Germany; communists seized power in Hungary briefly at the end of the war, communist and socialist parties won increasing support in elections in Portugal, Spain, France, Germany and Italy. At the same time frictions between Serbs, Croats and Slovenes destabilised the new state of Yugoslavia; tensions between Poles and Ukrainians caused problems in Poland; and the mix of nationalities in Czechoslovakia was a constant source of political difficulties.

Meanwhile the generation of 1914, and the returning soldiers in particular, had little faith in middle-class politicians or democracy. Democratic politics appeared bourgeois, comfortable, materialist and dull. Many ex-soldiers felt a sense of disillusionment and purposelessness now the war was over. The war had seemed to show the efficacy of action rather than words, of violence rather than reason. Soldiers had found a kind of camaraderie, of community, in the trenches which was lacking when they returned home. It was this camaraderie (*trincerismo*) that Mussolini was to latch onto in winning support for fascism in Italy.

Moreover, democracy seemed unable to cope with the post-war problems. Democratic governments came and went with startling rapidity in the post-war years. Between 1919 and 1922 Italy had five different Prime Ministers; the average life span of a government in post-war Germany was less than eight months. The process of democracy also seemed to highlight and give voice to the divisions in society. In particular it emphasised the differences between right and left and even gave a voice to those committed to overthrow democracy. Whatever Wilson's hopes of a 'world made safe for democracy', democracy was too delicate a flower to survive the hostile climate of post-war Europe unless – as in Britain and France – it was already well-rooted. In most places it was not.

Right-wing nationalism, as it had developed before the war and was to continue to develop after, was well placed to take advantage of these factors and soon attracted support from a wide swathe of public opinion. The First World War had shown the power of the national idea; its end had produced an outburst of national feeling – from national groups seeking statehood, from xenophobic cries for revenge on enemies, from a sense of national humiliation in defeat, from a sense of national injustice at a 'mutilated victory', from a desire to recover lands considered part of the national territory. The right argued that only it could defend the nation from its internal and external enemies. The right offered strength, leadership and unity in place of weakness and division; purpose and action in place of paralysis. In countries like Spain and Portugal, arguably, the right's greatest appeal lay in its opposition to communism and socialism. In central Europe, its appeal was the strong line taken against national minorities and Jews. Everywhere it was essentially anti-democratic and anti-liberal. Authoritarian government and loyalty to the state were the priorities.

b) Nationalism and Fascism

The most extreme forms of nationalism came to the fore in Italian Fascism and German Nazism. Both offered a seductive cocktail that played on fear of communism, disillusion with democracy and resentment at peace terms, alongside a vision of a purposeful, fulfilling future which would see the nation restored to its true greatness. Fascism and Nazism drew on the integral nationalism which had begun to develop before the First World War. Whatever their other features, what distinguishes these two movements is the central and prime importance of the nation. Liberals might espouse the idea of national self-determination, but only as a means of securing individual freedom; conservatives might appeal to nationalism in order to justify their claim to power or action against socialists. But for Fascists and Nazis what they were against and what they were for were defined in relation to the nation. They were anti-liberal because liberalism placed the individual above the nation; they were anti-communist because communism, by pitting class against class, threatened the unity of the nation. For Nazis, communism was also the product of a Marxist-Jewish conspiracy designed to sap Germany's strength. The nation gave meaning and purpose to people's lives: only through service to the nation could the individual achieve fulfilment.

So how did Fascists and Nazis view the nation? Consider the following extract from Mussolini, the Italian Fascist leader, speaking in Naples in October 1922:

1   We have created our myth.... Our myth is the nation, our myth is the greatness of the nation! And to this myth, this greatness, which we want to translate into a total reality, we subordinate everything else.

    For us the nation is not just territory, but something spiritual. There
5 are States which have had immense territories and which have left no trace in human history. It is not just a question of size, because there have been minute, microscopic States in history which have bequeathed memorable, immortal specimens of art and philosophy.

    The greatness of the nation is the totality of all these qualities, of all

10 these conditions. A nation is great when it translates into reality the force of its spirit. Rome becomes great when, starting out as a small rural democracy, it gradually spreads out across the whole of Italy in accordance with its spirit, till it encounters the warriors of Carthage and must fight them. Then, gradually, it bears its standards to the ends
15 of the earth, but at every turn the Roman Empire is the creation of the spirit, since the weapons were aimed not just by the arms of the Roman legionaries, but by their spirit. Now, therefore, we desire the greatness of the nation, both material and spiritual ...[4]

For Mussolini and the Italian Fascists, therefore, the nation meant more than just a linguistic or ethnic community. It was a community with a purpose, a community with the desire to achieve greatness. The national spirit beating in every Italian heart would enable Italy to achieve greatness by the common action of its people.

The Nazi vision of the nation also had some of these qualities – a spirit, and a sense of mission – but, for Nazis, the basis of the German nation was its racial character. We have seen how one theme running through German nationalism since the Napoleonic period was the sense of the uniqueness of the German people derived from its language, culture and the soil. Nationalists like Fichte had also argued that German culture and civilisation was superior. To this was added the pseudo-scientific idea derived from Gobineau and Chamberlain (see page 96) that the German people represented the purest elements of the Aryan race, racially superior to all other peoples.

Consider this extract from one of Hitler's speeches made in Munich in July 1922:

1 The Jew has never founded any civilisation, though he has destroyed hundreds. He possesses nothing of his own creation.... Foreign peoples, foreign workmen build him his temples; it is foreigners who create and work for him, it is foreigners who shed their blood for him.... He
5 does not even know how to preserve the precious things others have created.... In the last resort it is the Aryan alone who can form states and set them on their path to future greatness. All this the Jew cannot do. And because he cannot do it, therefore all his revolutions must be international. They must spread as a pestilence spreads. Already he has
10 destroyed Russia; now it is the turn of Germany, and with his envious instinct for destruction he seeks to disintegrate the national spirit of the Germans and to pollute their blood.[5]

The German *Volk* (people) had a duty and mission as the only culture-creating nation to protect its racial purity from contamination by inferior races, especially those which, it was argued, destroyed culture – the Jews, gypsies and Negroes. Nazism also demanded that the individual subordinate himself to the *Volk*. This idea is discussed by Hitler in the following extract from a speech made in October 1933:

1 National Socialism takes as the starting point of its views and its

decisions neither the individual nor humanity. It puts consciously into the central point of its whole thinking the *Volk*. This *Volk* is a blood-conditioned entity in which it sees the God-willed building-stone of human
5 society. The individual is transitory, the *Volk* is permanent.... National Socialism ... desires to safeguard the *Volk*, if necessary even at the expense of the individual ... above all [the individual] must realise that the freedom of the mind and will of the nation are to be valued more highly than the individual's freedom of mind and will.[6]

In order to achieve their respective national missions, Mussolini and Hitler both wanted to change the nature of Italians and Germans, producing people capable of carrying out their vision of the future. Both Fascism and Nazism took the idea of integral nationalism – the subordination of the individual to the needs of the nation – to its limits. The individual must be remoulded to serve the national will, be made to see that his life had no meaning except in service to that will. The interpreter of that will was the leader, the *Duce* or *Führer*, who, through his genius, had an intuitive understanding of it. All the individual had to do was obey. This was all neatly summed up in slogans like (in Nazi Germany) *Ein Reich! Ein Volk! Ein Führer!* (One state! One people! One leader!) or (in Fascist Italy) 'Believe! Obey! Fight!'

The latter slogan indicates another theme of these movements – the emphasis on struggle, martial spirit and war. Both Fascism and Nazism also drew heavily on Social Darwinist beliefs to argue that struggle between nations was natural and would determine the fittest to survive. The test of a nation was war and the conquest of empire; strong nations would survive, the weak would go under (Mussolini was careful to make sure the victims of his aggression were weaker!). Peace was unhealthy as it sapped the strength of the nation. Mussolini argued that a nation had to go to war at least once every 25 years in order to retain its vigour.

Mussolini established his Fascist regime in Italy after 1922 and Hitler came to power in 1933. Once in power, through propaganda, censorship, education, control of major institutions, and terror, they attempted to mould the nation. In foreign policy they sought to revise the settlement of 1919 and to pursue their imperial ambitions. Fascism and Nazism took nationalism to an extreme and certainly this version of nationalism was the antithesis of the liberal democratic version which Woodrow Wilson had hoped would take root in the new Europe.

As indicated above, there were right-wing regimes elsewhere and some mirrored Fascist Italy and Nazi Germany in relation to some of their policies. Intolerance of national minorities and the Jews was a feature of many eastern European regimes, such as that of Admiral Horthy in Hungary. Virulent opposition to communism was another common feature of right-wing dictatorships (as in Hungary and in Metaxas' Greece after 1936). Militant nationalism was a feature of the Hungarian regime and of Pilsudski's Polish regime (from 1926).

Some conservative right-wing dictators copied certain Fascist practices and many states had fascist-style parties.

6 Nationalism, Society and Economics

> **KEY ISSUE** To what extent did nationalism shape social and economic developments?

a) Social Policy

We have seen how before the First World War governments were becoming concerned about the health, mentally and physically, of the nation. In the general context of Social Darwinism, the issue was a crucial one for national survival. In the post-war period this was also true. Fears of national weakness were compounded by the losses of the First World War and long-term declines in birth-rates. Governments across Europe became concerned to promote healthy living and to increase the birth rate. The encouragement given to family life, and in particular to the role of women as mothers, was not simply the preserve of the fascist regimes in Italy and Germany. Their medals and incentives to have children and their propaganda promoting the family was mirrored in the French government's issuing of medals for large families and Stalin's promotion of the family in the 1930s. In English schools, girls were taught 'Infant Management' and 'Domestic Science'. The fascist slogan that 'Maternity is the patriotism of women' would not have been out of place in many states across Europe. Equally, the health of the nation was promoted through the encouragement of sport and organisations like the Boy Scouts.

b) Sport and National Symbols

In the inter-war period sport became the arena for competition between nations and through the mass media was followed by a national audience. Regular international football matches were seen as tests of national prestige. The first World Cup was held in 1930. The Olympic Games, revived in 1896, gathered momentum and in 1936 in Berlin became the test of the Nazi regime's attempts to prove the supremacy of the Aryan race. In one sense they achieved this – Germany won more medals than any other country. However, the Berlin games will always be remembered for the remarkable achievements of the black American Jesse Owens, who won four gold medals.

Eric Hobsbawm has argued that sport was – and is – a vital means for encouraging national feeling:

> What has made sport so uniquely effective a medium for inculcating national feelings ... is the ease with which even the least political or

public individuals can identify with the nation as symbolised by [sports-men].[7]

The symbolic importance of national teams and sportsmen was reflected also in the continued growth and importance of other national symbols which, in an age of radio and popular film-going, became increasingly part of everyday life. Interest in the British royal family, for instance, reached new heights and the Christmas Day radio broadcast by the King was instituted in 1932. Through the media of newspapers, film and radio, politicians could reach national audiences effectively and easily. This was a lesson fascist regimes learnt well. They did not underestimate the power of the media in promoting a national image and saw control and censorship of all the arts as a priority.

c) Economics and Economic Nationalism

During the First World War governments intervened in the running of their economies in an unprecedented way in order to marshal the state's resources for the war effort. Industry and agriculture, like citizens, had to work in the national interest. At the end of the war this process was more or less discontinued, despite pressures from the left to retain state control. However, a return to free trade was difficult because of the severe disruption caused by the war. European states had lost many of their overseas markets and many of the economies were crippled with debt. What is more the economies of the new states created in the peace were fragile. In this atmosphere of economic crisis it is not surprising that the new nation states sought protection for their own industries through the imposition of tariff barriers. This kind of economic nationalism, rather than free trade, was a hallmark of the inter-war period that was exacerbated by the effects of the Wall Street Crash. In the early 1930s even the free trade nation *par excellence*, Great Britain, adopted a semi-protectionist stance by introducing Imperial Preference – a favoured status given to trade with the British Empire – and imposed tariffs on foreign goods. Everywhere the Depression intensified the moves towards economic nationalism. Tariff barriers were raised to fend off foreign competition and countries sought to find salvation in self-sufficiency. Inevitably this meant governments becoming more involved in economic affairs – in repudiating debt, in protecting key industries, in subsidising farmers.

To some extent the fascist states had led the way in economic nationalism by trying to subordinate the economy to the perceived needs of the nation. In Italy the approach was not systematic, but initially consisted of a series of 'battles' – the 'battle for grain' and the 'battle for the lira', for example. Mussolini also sought to direct the economy and control the workers through the setting up of 'corporations' representing employers, workers and the state, but even here there was little systematic planning. This was partly because Mussolini, like Hitler, saw the economic progress as a means to an end, not an end in itself. In Nazi Germany there was some attempt at economic planning in the New Plan, which was then supplanted by the Four Year Plan to prepare Germany for war. Whilst there was no attempt to take over private enterprises, it was made clear to industry that the state's protection was dependent on industry serving the needs of the nation.

7 Nationalism and the Second World War

> **KEY ISSUES** What was the influence of nationalism on international affairs? What impact did nationalism have on the nature of the Second World War?

When Woodrow Wilson envisaged a Europe of democratic nation states he hoped that the recognition of national aspirations would ease the tensions on the continent and allow the development of a new world order based on mutual respect between nation states and guaranteed by cooperation in a League of Nations which would resolve disputes peacefully through negotiation. Yet, as noted earlier, the peace settlements left 30 millions outside their 'national' home and gave practically every new state, as well as the defeated powers, a sense of grievance which would be a major force for destabilising international relations. Just as nationalists in Italy before the war wanted to incorporate their *irredenta* into the united Italy, now Poles wanted to annex Vilna, Teschen and lands to the east, Hungarians wanted to recover lands given to Czechoslovakia, Bulgaria wanted to recover lands from Romania, Germany wanted to recover the Polish Corridor, and Austria wanted to unite with Germany.

Moreover, once it became clear that the USA would not join the League, Britain's and France's commitment distinctly cooled. For both, their own national interests would, when in conflict, always override international action. France, for instance, insecure about Germany, decided not to rely on the League's paper guarantees of collective security and instead sought to make defensive alliances with the new nation states to the east of Germany. When Germany reneged on her reparations payments, France ignored international opinion and invaded the Ruhr (1923) to seize by force what she was owed. Without regard to international opinion, Poland seized Vilna from Lithuania and sought to take advantage of Russian weakness by invading her in 1920. Soon after he came to power in 1922, Mussolini, too, flexed his muscles in pursuit of national prestige. In 1923 he picked a quarrel with Greece over the shooting of an Italian General on the Albanian border. However, as the immediate post-war problems faded and some kind of economic stability returned, a more stable if still fragile period of international relations ensued in the second half of the 1920s, symbolised by the Locarno Treaties of 1925 which brought Germany back into the international fold.

The Treaty of Versailles had left Germany with a deep sense of grievance and all inter-war governments in Germany sought a revision of its terms. After the issue of France's invasion of the Ruhr was peacefully resolved in 1924, the new German foreign minister, Gustav Stresemann, sought the gradual revision of the Versailles treaty by negotiation. His priorities initially were the reduction of reparations and the removal of Allied forces from the Rhineland, but he also hoped for a revision of Germany's eastern frontiers. His untimely death in 1929 and the onset of Depression stopped this peaceful revisionism. With the rise of Hitler in Germany and with an increasingly aggressive Mussolini in Italy, along with the collapse of democracy across eastern Europe, expansionist nationalism once more threatened European peace. For both Mussolini and Hitler, an aggressive foreign policy was bound up with their vision of the nation. For Mussolini, the dream was the creation of a new Roman Empire; for Hitler, the creation of a Greater Germany to encompass all of the German *Volk* and then the conquest of *lebensraum* (living space) at the expense of inferior races to the east.

Mussolini began his expansion in 1935 when Italian forces invaded the independent African state of Abyssinia. Success here, and the successful defiance of the League of Nations, was followed by expensive and less than glorious support for General Franco and the nationalists in the Spanish Civil War, the annexation of Albania (1939) and the invasion of France in June 1940 (just before its defeat by Germany). The invasion of Abyssinia, perhaps more than any other event, proved the hollowness of the League of Nations concept of collective security and encouraged aggressive nationalism in other states, especially Germany.

War, for Hitler, was the function of the nation as it fought for living space. The quest for empire was the test of the nation's virility. Hitler had said in 1930: 'Every creature strives to expand and every nation strives for global mastery. Only those who keep this goal in view are on the right road'.[8] Although there is debate about how detailed a plan Hitler had in terms of foreign policy, Hitler had three (or possibly four) general aims in view: freeing Germany from the shackles imposed by Versailles (achieved by 1936 when Hitler had begun to rearm and had re-militarised the Rhineland); the creation of a German-dominated central Europe with an enlarged Germany containing all German nationals, broadly the *Grossdeutsch* Germany dreamed of in the 1840s (achieved by 1939); then a drive eastwards to conquer living-space (begun in 1939 and with renewed vigour with the invasion of Russia in 1941); and finally, some historians argue, world domination.

The pursuit of revision of the terms of Versailles and then the uniting of Austrian and Sudeten Germans in a greater Germany did not bring war. This can partly be explained by influential British views that the Treaty of Versailles was unjust toward Germany and that all Germany wanted was the application of the principle of national self-determination that had been denied in 1919. Certainly it was only when Hitler went beyond this by occupying the rest of Czechoslovakia in March 1939 that Britain and France decided the German dictator had gone too far. It is also worth noting that Poland and Hungary also took advantage of the lack of British and French support for Czechoslovakia to seize their *irredenta* in Teschen and the south.

The Second World War started when the extreme nationalist policies of Germany led to the invasion of Poland in September 1939. The war was of a different character from that of 1914–18. Whilst there were the same calls for the defence of the homeland and for even greater total mobilisation of the nation, this was a war in the west much more obviously about the defence of freedom and democracy against the evils of Nazism than about national or imperial rivalry. Interestingly, however, after 1941, Stalin did play the patriotic card. The Soviet Union's war was depicted as the Great Patriotic War rather than a defence of communism.

8 Conclusion

KEY ISSUE What was the nature of inter-war nationalism?

The inter-war period had been shaped decisively by the peace settlements of 1919–20 and the economic, political and social dislocations caused by four years of slaughter. However, the tragedy of the First World War had not drawn the sting of nationalism. Rather it had, perhaps, reinforced it. National minorities had been encouraged to press their claims and the settlements made left both winners or losers dissatisfied. In addition the idea that the introduction of a new democratic system of government would still aggressive voices, reconcile people to accept the peace settlement and pacify rival nationalities proved false. Indeed democracy seemed only to accentuate internal divisions, reinforcing the call for strong authoritarian governments that would impose national unity and seek redress of international grievances. Fear of communism and the failure of democratic governments to deal with intense economic problems ensured even more support for right-wing nationalist solutions.

These solutions had not come out of the blue. They drew on the right-wing nationalism that had developed before the war, especially the integral or ultra nationalism which placed loyalty to the nation above all else and promoted intolerance to all rival loyalties and perceived enemies of the nation. Nazism and Fascism can in this sense be seen as a logical extension of developments in pre-war nationalism. For liberal nationalists like Woodrow Wilson, national self-determination was espoused as a means to the end of securing liberal democracy. However, Hitler and Mussolini portrayed the nation as an end in itself.

When Nazism was defeated in 1945, nationalism was to take a back seat in questions of peace and the new world order. The shape of post-war politics for over 40 years was to be dominated in Europe not by questions of nationalism, but by the Cold War between liberal democracy and capitalism on the one side and Soviet-style communism on the other, even if these can be seen as aspects of American or Soviet nationalism.

References

1 As quoted in C. Thorne, *Ideology and Power* (Collier-Macmillan, 1965) p. 180.

2 M. Mazower, *Dark Continent: Europe's Twentieth Century* (Penguin, 1998) p. 49.

3 M. McCauley, *Stalin and Stalinism* (Longman, 1995) p. 110.

4 Mussolini, 'The Naples Speech, 24 October 1922', as quoted in R. Griffin, *Fascism* (Oxford, 1995), p. 44.

5 From a speech at Munich, 28 July 1922 as quoted in A. Bullock, *Hitler: A Study in Tyranny* (Penguin, 1962) p. 407.

6 Hitler's speech at the Nazi Harvest Thanksgiving Celebrations at Buckeburg, 7 October 1933, as quoted in Bullock, *Hitler: A Study in Tyranny*, p. 401.

7 E.J. Hobsbawm, *Nations and Nationalism since 1780* (Cambridge, 1990), p. 143.

8 As quoted in H. Schulze, *States, Nations and Nationalism* (Blackwell, 1996) p. 300.

Summary Diagram

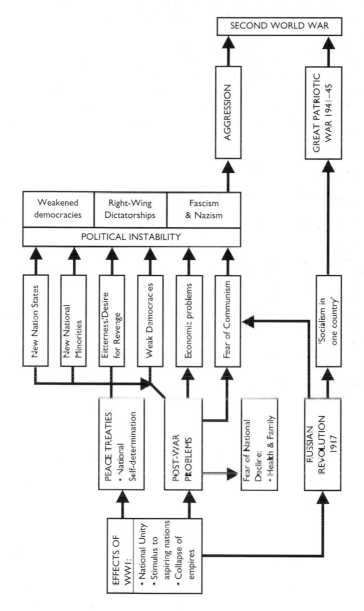

1. Nationalism, Fascism and Nazism

Read the extracts quoted on pages 120–22 and answer the following questions:

a) Examine Mussolini's speech on pages 120–21. Why do you think that Mussolini referred to the Roman Empire? (*3 marks*)

b) How useful is the extract from Mussolini's Naples Speech as evidence of Mussolini's view of the nation? (*6 marks*)

c) How reliable is the extract from Hitler's Munich speech on page 121 about Nazi attitudes to race? (*6 marks*)

d) Compare and contrast Hitler's speech from 1933 on pages 121–22 with Mussolini's Naples speech as evidence of fascist views of the nation. (*10 marks*)

Advice: AS and A-level questions often ask students to comment on the utility or reliability of sources as evidence of a particular aspect of the topic. Whilst students can learn a list of more or less relevant questions to ask of a source (Who wrote it? When? Who for? and so on), the key to a good answer is how far the student can use the answers to such questions in order to draw valid conclusions about the questions set.

a) This type of question is seeking to examine your ability to use your knowledge of the historical context to explain the reference. In this case you need to think about why Mussolini referred to the Roman Empire in his speech and not some other empire.

b) The question wants an assessment of the utility of the source as evidence of Mussolini's view of the nation. The first question to ask then, is what information does it give about Mussolini's view of the nation? A lot? Or a little? Is the main focus of the document the nation? Next consider the authorship: does this lend to or detract from the credibility of the views expressed? What type of source is it? Will that have any bearing on its credibility or suggest what a historian might use the source as an example of? (A source may be flawed in all kinds of ways and still be useful for particular purposes.) What of the date? Is that of any significance? Finally, and very importantly, how far do the views expressed fit in with what else is known about Mussolini's view of the state? A good answer will cover the ground that is most relevant to the question and will not simply go slavishly through a checklist of points. It will focus on the strengths and weaknesses of this source for the purpose required.

c) Again your answer must focus in on reliability (accuracy, typicality, completeness) for the purpose stated. The same questions as those above can be asked, but remember the focus this time is reliability, not use.

d) This is more demanding, requiring careful analysis of both sources, not just in what they say, but also as evidence. You have, of course assessed the Naples speech already, but now you must compare. The key to a good answer here is to ensure that comparisons are being made throughout. In what ways are the sources similar and in what ways different? Do the sources indicate key aspects of the nation, or only marginal ones? Do they give a complete or merely a partial view? Is their usefulness as sources affected by the fact that both are extracts from speeches?

Essay questions on Chapter 6

Consider the following A-level essay titles which include nationalism as a central theme:

1. To what extent and why was nationalism the most important element in the appeal of *either* Fascism in Italy *or* Nazism in Germany?
2. To what extent was fascism anything more than extreme nationalism?
3. Why was Wilson's principle of national self-determination unable to produce political stability in Europe after 1919?

Both questions 1 and 2 require you to examine the relationship between nationalism and fascism. For example, in question 1 the role of nationalism in the appeal of Fascism/Nazism has to be set against other elements of their appeal, such as the stand against communism and weak democracy or the attractions of strong leadership and the promise of solutions to the problems facing the state. One might argue, of course, that nationalism underpinned much of the wider appeal of the two movements. For example, the restoration of national pride required strong leadership and an attack on internationalist philosophies like communism.

Question 3 focuses directly on the issue of national self-determination. It requires you to consider the factors undermining political stability after 1919 but in a quite specific way. Relevant questions to think about include: could Wilson's principle, however applied, have provided political stability? Was it the way in which it was applied to central Europe in 1919–1920 which undermined its effectiveness in healing divisions? Was the denial of national self-determination to Germans in certain areas a major cause of political instability? Were other causes of instability simply too great?

In addition to the above style of questions, consideration of nationalism will form an element of many A-level essay answers to questions considering political developments in particular states, such as Italy, Germany, and France, or to questions considering international relations, especially those focusing on the breakdown of international peace in the 1930s.

7 Conclusion: The Significance of Nationalism

POINTS TO CONSIDER

This chapter draws some of the basic themes together and poses some questions about nationalism at the end of the twentieth century. The key aim is for you to reflect on what you have studied and consider its relevance for today.

1 Reflections

KEY ISSUE How far did the nature of nationalism change between 1789 and 1945?

In the introduction to this book I suggested that the terms nation and nationalism were difficult to define precisely. Clearly at different times and in different places and amongst different groups the definition of the nation and the nature of nationalism has varied. But certain key developments do seem to have occurred. For the first part of this period, up to and including 1848, nationalism took the form of a largely middle-class movement, strongest amongst intellectuals and students, especially aiming at creating a nation state with a liberal constitution. The link with liberalism was strong because ideas of popular sovereignty and equal rights for citizens dovetailed with a view of nationalism that opposed the autocratic rulers of both multi-national empires (Habsburg, Ottoman) and minor states (as in the German Confederation and the Italian peninsula). This liberal link was revived, briefly, in the Wilsonian euphoria at the end of the First World War that saw an attempt to create a Europe of liberal democratic nation states.

Exactly how important nationalism was before 1848 is open to dispute, but certainly it failed in central Europe. Where it succeeded – in Belgium and Greece – nationalist movements had the support of the Great Powers. The revolutionaries of 1848 had no such support. The realities of power politics brought home to liberals and nationalists the lesson that without power little could be achieved.

When nation states were created in the next period (1848–1878), the role of nationalism and nationalist movements is open to question. It is possible to build a reasonably convincing explanation of the unification of Germany, for instance, with minimal reference to national movements. Indeed most nationalists were against Prussia in 1866 – until it won! But did nationalism play only a minimal part? Why then was a German Empire created in 1871 and not simply an expanded Prussia? Why was a kingdom of Italy declared and not an expanded Piedmont? What does seem to be clear, both in the case of Italy and Germany and in the case of the independent Balkan states, is that the creation of nation states depended for success on the support of, or acquiescence of, existing great powers. It also depended on the relative weakness of Austria (in central Europe) and the Ottoman Empire (in the Balkans). The efforts of nationalists alone were insufficient.

Once nation states were created, governments tried to create nations out of the mass of the people. States adopted a variety of means to create a sense of national unity and loyalty amongst the masses. But as peoples developed a national consciousness, inevitably state policy had to take account of public perceptions of the national interest. These perceptions could be shaped and exploited both by governments and by other political forces, such as the extreme right. Nationalism, for example, could be turned against the class antagonisms and internationalism encouraged by socialism and also against the apparent threat to national unity posed by national minorities. Across Europe nationalism was hijacked by the right, influenced by Social Darwinist ideas about national strength and struggles for survival. Such ideas informed the dash for empire in the last quarter of the nineteenth century and the quest for military power in the years before 1914. Certainly the acquisition of colonies, the defence of national interest abroad and the size of armies (and navies) became the litmus tests of national prestige and greatness. But the exact nature and degree of influence exerted by such nationalism remains a matter of debate. As with the process of making nation states, the role of nationalism is not always easy to disentangle from a range of other developments and pressures. Certainly the popular demonstrations of August 1914 seem to show that a sense of nationalism and national pride had permeated the masses. The lack of significant popular opposition to the war until 1917–18 also testifies to a remarkable degree of national unity in the face of a common enemy.

The rightward drift of nationalism continued after the war despite the hopes that national self-determination would produce a stable liberal democratic Europe. The ultra-nationalist vision peddled by Fascists and Nazis was seductive enough to bring them mass support in the climate of economic crises, political uncertainty, fear of communism and post-war bitterness. Fascists sought to persuade Italians that the interests of the nation and the need to make Italy great took precedence over all other priorities. Nazis sought to persuade Germans of their racial mission and their right to military conquest at the expense of 'inferior' races. In comparison to the nation the individual was meaningless. The national will as interpreted by the leader was all that mattered. The result of such beliefs was another world war, more devastating than the first.

Nationalism, then, over this period, wore many different clothes. Even communism was nationalised in Stalin's Soviet Union. It helped shape events and was in turn shaped by them. But what remained, even after 1945, was the acceptance of the national idea, the principle of national self-determination and the political organisation of the nation state.

2 Nationalism in Europe After 1945

> **KEY ISSUE** To what extent is nationalism still relevant today?

Understandably, perhaps, in the light of the Nazi experience and the pressures of the Cold War, nationalism lost some of its centrality in Europe after the Second World War, except perhaps on the sports field, where national passions could be quickly aroused. It is worth noting, however, that, in western Europe at least, the nation state has remained liberal and democratic. Outside Europe nationalism remained a potent force, however, as colonies sought and gained independence (ironically, given European nationalism's hostility to socialism, often supported by socialist and Marxist groups opposed to 'capitalist imperialism').

Yet nationalism has in recent years again become prominent. At the end of the twentieth century it seemed as potent a force in Europe as it was at the century's start. Indeed there are now more 'nation states' than ever before, and there exist pressures both in eastern and western Europe for the creation of even more. Both Scottish and Welsh nationalism have undergone something of a revival since the 1970s and many fear that the granting of devolved powers to a Scottish parliament and a Welsh Assembly is merely the stepping stone to the break-up of the United Kingdom. The problem of Ireland remains unresolved and one can only hope that the sectarian violence that has been such a feature of Ulster politics since 1969 will not continue into the twenty-first century. Elsewhere the Basques (who have also used violence) still press for recognition in Spain, Germany has been re-united, Czechoslovakia has split into the Czech and Slovak republics, and Yugoslavia has disintegrated into separate states. In the wake of the old Soviet Union, Latvia, Lithuania and Estonia are once more independent, and Georgia, Belorussia and a number of other independent states have emerged. Whilst in many cases the transitions have been relatively peaceful, the break-up of the Yugoslav state has been accompanied by warfare and Russia has been involved in an internal war against the Chechens. Economic problems and the strength of national feeling still threaten to bring about militant nationalist governments like that of Slobodan Milosevic in Serbia.

Whilst all of the above are examples of nations seeking or winning liberation or independence, there has also been a worrying revival of right-wing nationalism in relatively stable states like France, Austria, Italy and Germany. In France, Austria and Germany the targets of this nationalism are the immigrant communities, whilst in Italy there has been a move to create a North Italian state.

But since the end of the Second World War, war between individual states in western Europe has seemed a remote possibility. A key reason for this is the development of international organisations making western European states mutually dependent. The North Atlantic Treaty Organisation has offered effective collective security whilst the European Community (now European Union) has bound states together in key areas of economic and social policy. However, the supposed threat of a European super-state arguably implicit in increased cooperation has led to some revival of nationalist feeling expressed as a concern for the loss of national sovereignty. Nationalism threatens to flourish in the twenty-first century as it flourished in the nineteenth and twentieth.

How can we explain the resilience of the national idea? Is it due to its chameleon-like nature, changing its political colours to suit the circumstances? Or is it that the idea of the nation fulfils a human need for a sense of belonging to a wider community in an industrial and complex age? Ernest Renan, the French historian, clearly saw great value in the national idea but still viewed nationalism as the product of the age whose time would pass. In his lecture in 1882 in answer to the question 'What is a nation?' he suggested that:

1 Human desires change; but what does not change on this earth? Nations are not something eternal. They have begun, they will end. They will be replaced, in all probability, by a European confederation. But such is not the law of the century in which we live. At the present
5 time the existence of nations happens to be good, even necessary. Their existence is a guarantee of liberty, which would be lost if the world had only one law and only one master.[1]

What do you think?

References

1   F. Renan, *Qu'est-ce qu'une nation?* as quoted in J. Hutchinson & A.D. Smith (eds), *Nationalism* (Oxford, 1994) pp. 17–18.

Further Reading

There is a good deal of specialist literature on nationalism but relatively little which is readily accessible to the general reader or sixth form student. I have picked out texts therefore of three kinds: general texts which will take the reader further than this general introduction, texts dealing with particular states, and texts on the theory of nationalism. I would recommend as a starting point, however, for gaining a clear knowledge of what happened when and an introduction to the areas of debate, L.W. Cowie and R. Wolfson, *Years of Nationalism 1815–1890* (Hodder & Stoughton, 1985) and R. Wolfson and J. Laver, *Years of Change Europe 1890–1945* (Hodder & Stoughton, 1996). There are also the relevant books in the Access series, such as A. Stiles, *Napoleon, France and Europe* (1993), *The Unification of Italy 1815–70* (1996), and *The Unification of Germany 1815–90* (1989); K. Randell, *France: The Third Republic 1870–1914* (1991); M. Robson, *Italy: Liberalism and Fascism 1870–1945* (1992); and R. Pearce, *Fascism and Nazism* (1997).

General texts:
Timothy Baycroft, *Nationalism in Europe 1789–1945* (CUP, 1998) offers a general introduction which is theoretical in nature. Hagen Schulze, *States, Nations and Nationalism From the Middle Ages to the Present* (Blackwell, 1996) offers a relatively accessible and clear overview of the interaction between nationalism and events. Alan Cassels, *Ideology and International Relations in the Modern World* (Routledge, 1996) provides a useful and readable overview of the relationship between nationalism (and other ideologies) and international affairs. R. Gildea's *Barricades and Borders, Europe 1800–1914* (Oxford, 1996), whilst a general history of Europe, has nationalism as a central theme. There are useful and provocative chapters in the four volumes on modern history by E.J. Hobsbawm, all published by Abacus, *The Age of Revolution 1789–1848* (1962), *The Age of Capital 1848–1878* (1975), *The Age of Empire 1878–1914* (1987), and *The Age of Extremes* (1994), and a more demanding but focused approach in the same author's *Nations and Nationalism since 1780* (CUP, 1990). All place developments in nationalism in a world context. There are useful essays on individual states in M. Teich and R. Porter, *The National Question in Europe in Historical Context* (CUP, 1993). M. Broers, *Europe after Napoleon, Revolution, Reaction and Romanticism, 1814–1848* (Manchester University Press, 1996) sets the role of nationalism in the context of other ideological developments.

Theory:
There is a vast and growing literature on the theory of nationalism. Much of this is quite difficult for the general reader but the following are useful texts. P. Alter, *Nationalism* (Edward Arnold, 1989), Benedict

Anderson, *Imagined Communities* (Verso, 1991), J. Breuilly, *Nationalism and the State* (Manchester University Press, 1993), and E. Gellner, *Nationalism* (Pheonix,1997). There are two useful and stimulating collections: *Nationalism*, edited by John Hutchinson and Anthony D. Smith (OUP, 1994) brings together writing on nationalism by a range of prominent academics, whilst S. Woolf, *Nationalism in Europe 1815 to the present: a reader* (Routledge, 1996) is a similar collection which ranges from J.S. Mill (1861) to G.A. Williams (1979).

Texts on individual states:
Almost any history of a European state in the period 1789–1945 is going to mention nationalism. One, which also contains a selection of relevant documentary material is Hagen Schulze, *The Course of German Nationalism from Frederick the Great to Bismarck* (CUP, 1991). More directed at A-level students is the excellent W.G. Shreeves, *Nationmaking in Nineteenth Century Europe* (Nelson, 1984) which focuses on Italian and German unification and also contains useful primary material. Other specific works on Germany which are useful and take the reader beyond A-level texts, include W. Carr, *A History of Germany 1815–1990* (Arnold, 1991), which is a very good survey of German History, M. Hughes, *Nationalism and Society: Germany 1800–1945* (Arnold, 1988), in which, as the title suggests, nationalism is a central issue, and John Breuilly (ed.) *The State of Germany* (Longman, 1992) in which several academic historians contribute on the theme of nationalism.

On Italy I suggest H. Hearder and D.P. Waley (ed.s) *A Short History of Modern Italy* (CUP, 1966), H. Hearder, *Italy in the Age of the Risorgimento 1790–1870* (Longman, 1983) and Denis Mack Smith, *Modern Italy: a political history* (Yale, 1997). On France Robert Tombs, *France 1814–1914* (Longman, 1996) is excellent, marrying a thematic approach with a chronological section. J.P.T. Bury, *France 1814–1940* (Methuen, 1969) provides a solid clear narrative. For the Austrian Empire A. Sked, *The Decline and Fall of the Habsburg Empire 1815–1918* (Longman, 1989) is very useful. For Ireland, D. George Boyce, *Nationalism in Ireland* (Routledge, 1995) is a good introduction.

Index